Dear Stephanie,

Dear Paul

Dear Stephanie,

Dear Paul

✦

A Transatlantic Love Story Told Through
the Correspondence of Stephanie Grant
and Paul M. Duke, 1948–1949

Paul M. Duke
Stephanie Duke

*To Carol —
happy reading!
Stephanie*

iUniverse, Inc.
New York Lincoln Shanghai

Dear Stephanie, Dear Paul
A Transatlantic Love Story Told Through the Correspondence of Stephanie Grant and Paul M. Duke, 1948–1949

iUniverse books may be ordered through booksellers or by contacting:

iUniverse
2021 Pine Lake Road, Suite 100
Lincoln, NE 68512
www.iuniverse.com
1-800-Authors (1-800-288-4677)

ISBN-13: 978-0-595-39505-7 (pbk)
ISBN-13: 978-0-595-67719-1 (cloth)
ISBN-10: 0-595-39505-8 (pbk)
ISBN-10: 0-595-67719-3 (cloth)

Printed in the United States of America

To all Pen Friends:

Past, Present, and Future

Contents

About Dear Stephanie, Dear Paul:

Early in the spring of 1948, Stephanie Grant, a sixteen-year-old shorthand typist in England, submitted her name to a London newspaper that offered to advertise for pen friends in the American Midwest. In Akron, Ohio, Paul Duke, an eighteen-year-old college student who had left school to work as a construction laborer, happened on the advertisement and felt inspired to respond.

Thus began a pen pal relationship that lasted for a full year and resulted in the two writers meeting in person. This correspondence comprises the first part of *Dear Stephanie, Dear Paul*. Anyone who has ever had a pen friend will recognize certain features of this kind of letter writing. The early letters contain an exchange of biographical information and photographs, and reveal a number of personal and cultural prejudices. As the writers come to know and accept each other, they do indeed become friends and the exchange of letters becomes a valued routine in their lives. When other activities or the lack of a muse cause occasional lapses, there are appropriate scolds and apologies, and the correspondence resumes its normal pace.

What makes this particular set of letters compelling is that they document a full year in the lives of two young people approaching adulthood. To each other they reveal their hopes and fears, even as they attempt to present themselves as secure and sophisticated individuals. With a common interest in current events, reading, theatre, and music, there is always something new and exciting to write about. There are references to 1940s films, radio programs, advertising, fads, and the latest fashions. Stephanie is earning a weekly wage of £3.15.0 ($15), and Paul is taking home $50 or more in his weekly paycheck.

Historic events of the day are duly reported. Stephanie describes such things as the closing ceremonies of the Olympic Games in London, and the announcement by Prime Minister Clement Atlee of the new National Health System for Britain. Paul writes about the American presidential election and a campaign visit to Akron by President Harry S. Truman.

Memories of World War II (which had ended three years previously in 1945) were still fresh on both sides of the Atlantic. In America, the ten-year Great

Depression had been relieved by the growth of jobs in industry and agriculture required by the war effort. Paul's parents had seen three of their four boys march off to war and return safely home. But wartime food and fuel rationing had been slight, and with a booming postwar economy, the Duke family was prosperous enough to live in a large and comfortable house on Hazel Street and drive a luxurious new Ford Mercury automobile.

Throughout Europe, the postwar years were a time of worry and concern for populations struggling to rebuild their bombed cities, and trying to cope with critical shortages of goods and services. Wartime food and fuel rationing was still in effect, and harsh government policies curtailed supplies of electricity and gas to homes and workplaces.

In England, prosperity seemed an unattainable dream. The war left thousands of widows to cope on their own, and Stephanie's mother was one of them. The family home was sold and her mother went to work to support her two children in rented rooms. In 1946, the school leaving age was 15, and it was time for Stephanie to leave school and find work. She found employment in London as a junior typist and a home at the Cecil Residential Club on Gower Street, near the edge of Bloomsbury.

On the world scene, fears of another world war were everywhere—this time between Western democracies and the developing "Red Menace" of the Soviet Union. In 1946, Winston Churchill coined the phrase, "Iron Curtain," to describe the Soviet domination of Eastern Europe. In 1947, the Truman Doctrine and the Marshall Plan provided guaranteed help to nations threatened by communism. Tensions heightened also with the creation of the state of Israel in 1948, and the emergence of China as a communist nation.

The very real possibility of another world war was constantly in the news and on people's minds. Paul and Stephanie both take note of the danger, but war fears were largely overshadowed by the sheer joy of being on the brink of adulthood and having their first taste of independence from the restrictions of home and school.

A second set of letters, written following Paul's first visit to England in 1949, occupies Part II of this book. The long, tentative courtship-by-mail quality of the pen pal letters is now replaced by more sober reflection as Paul and Stephanie attempt to come to terms with what has happened to them after that idyllic month they spent together in England. Is it love? For that matter, as Stephanie wants to know, "What *is* love?" And what are they going to do about it? What does the future hold for them?

A Note on the Editing:

The number and length of the original letters had to be greatly reduced in order to present them in a publishable state. Here and there I have added a few clarifying words or sentences to eliminate the need for distracting footnotes. Misspellings have been silently corrected, and English/American spelling variations have been allowed to stand just as we wrote them. The guiding rule always was to preserve the flavor and essential details of the original letters for the pleasure of the general reader.

P.M.D.

Part One:
Pen Pals

During the pre-television years immediately following World War II, international pen pal correspondence was a popular hobby in many parts of the world. It was a way of expanding horizons, improving writing and language skills, and there was always the hope of one day visiting another country and having the benefit of a friend in that foreign land.

Most such correspondence was short-lived. Language barriers or the distractions of everyday living often proved to be inhibiting factors, and if it became obvious that neither writer was likely to visit the other in the foreseeable future, the exchange of letters was apt to wither and die.

The letters that follow represent a pen pal correspondence that did continue to a satisfactory ending. In sum they provide a unique record of more than a year and a half in each of our young lives—an evocative glimpse of a vanished era—an overture to our future.

How did it all begin? By chance—by some unseen hand of fate. Early in March of 1948, Stephanie Grant, just out of school and working as a shorthand typist in London, happened to purchase a newspaper, the London Daily Mail, *that featured an article on the American Midwest. The writer urged British readers to become better acquainted with Americans and offered to advertise for pen friends in the overseas edition of the newspaper. Because of her interest in America, Stephanie decided to send in her name.*

Meanwhile, in Akron, Ohio, as a result of listening to the short-wave broadcasts of the BBC, I had developed an interest in all things British. One evening in early April—about a month after Stephanie submitted her name—I stopped by the local news exchange in Akron to see what British publications might be for sale. I selected several magazines and a recent edition of The Overseas Mail.

Returning home with these treasures and prepared for a full evening of reading, I never got beyond the third page of the Mail. *There, in the upper right-hand corner, I noticed a headline: REQUESTS FOR PEN FRIENDS. As I looked down at the list of possible correspondents, somehow my eye never strayed far from one particular entry: "Surrey girl, 16, Reading and the Theatre." With all the energy and enthusiasm of an eighteen-year-old, I put down the paper and raced across the room to my typewriter...*

April 10, 1948
Greetings from America!

Greetings at least from a red-blooded American youth of the Midwest. My name is Paul, and my age is 18.

First of all, I must say that I hope you get a favorable impression of me from this letter, as I would like very much to have you as a regular correspondent.

You say you are interested in reading and the theatre. I wonder if you have ever read any of the books of the American author Thomas Wolfe? If you haven't, may I suggest him as the best possible introduction to this country? He is very poetic and isn't afraid to use big words, but I don't think you'll have any trouble understanding him.

Someday before too long, I hope to come to England. I guess farther fields look greener, but I have always felt that England would be a better place to live than America. One example of British superiority is in radio. I listen quite regularly to the BBC, and I find it much better than American radio.

I think I'll let this letter end here, but upon assurances of continued correspondence from you, I shall be only too happy to pour out thousands of words into letters. And I guarantee they will come often!

Waiting and hoping to hear from you soon,
Paul M. Duke
696 Hazel Street
Akron 5, Ohio, U.S.A.
The World, The Universe,
???????????

◆   ◆   ◆

Cecil Residential Club
195-201 Gower Street
London N.W.1., England
22nd April 1948
Dear Paul,

Britain returns greetings to America, at least I do, and it amounts to much the same thing. Your letter interested me very much and I do hope you will keep your promise to pour out thousands of words into letters. Yes, I am very interested in reading, but I'm ashamed to say that I haven't read many American authors. In fact, the only one I can think of is John Steinbeck—I think his books are marvelous. Please don't think me too awful, but I haven't read any of Thomas Wolfe's works. I have entered him on my library list though, and will certainly take up your suggestion and get to know him.

My name is Stephanie, and I will be 17 in August. My home is in Epsom, Surrey, about 25 miles away from London. I have just started being a shorthand-typist with a firm in London. To be near my work, I live at a girls' club and journey home at the weekend.

I'm sure you will like England when you come. I think most Americans do, but I haven't heard of them wanting to live here. We are so much slower than you. Why I am sure I am right in saying that only about a quarter of the houses in Britain have hot running water, and only about half have baths installed. I expect that seems shocking to you, but over here it is the normal way of life and people don't seem to want it any different.

I was surprised to read of your preference of British radio. I can never complain enough of our BBC. We get only a few good programmes and the rest a lot of third-rate variety shows or record programmes.

I suppose living in the Middle West you do not have as much opportunity for theatre going as one living in New York. Or am I wrong? I have seen several of Laurence Olivier's productions in London, including *King Lear* and *Richard III*. A little while ago I saw the musical *Annie Get Your Gun*, and thought it was marvelous. I found it impossible to get into see Danny Kaye at his recent London appearance. I queued and queued for seats, but it was in vain. We have had quite a tidal wave of American variety stars of late—good and bad—including Mickey Rooney, The Ink Spots, Martha Raye, and Carmen Miranda. But I haven't seen any of them.

Have you been to the ballet at all? I think it is beautiful to watch. I love music, do you?

Next time you write, please tell me something about what you do and all about Akron. You have my promise, practically written in blood (except that it hurts too much), that I will write regularly as soon as I hear from you.

Yours sincerely, Stephanie Grant

◆   ◆   ◆

Akron, Ohio
April 27, 1948
Dear Stephanie,

Exactly three weeks, two days, twenty-two hours and ten seconds after I mailed my letter to you, I received your welcome reply.

Effective immediately, I intend to write much and often. It's probably too much to expect you to write as often as I will, but do as well as you can.

As to the town I live in, the city of Akron (known as "The Rubber Capital of The World") is far from the best as cities go in this country, and I had the misfortune of being born here. My mother's family originally came from Wales, and my father's family came from England. Dad is a bricklayer/stonemason and has always managed to take care of us financially over the years—even during the Great Depression. There are four "kids" and I am "the baby." My oldest brother Ted is head of the classics department at the University of Akron. Next is Bruce, who will shortly be getting a master's degree in chemistry. Then there is Richard, who is in the army—he re-enlisted after serving during the War. We are about four years apart in age.

Last fall, I started at Akron University, but after one semester decided to take time out and decide just what I want to do with the rest of my life. I will be going back to work as a construction laborer for now—it may sound like hard work, but the $1.10 an hour pay is more than I can get anywhere else without special training.

It's tough to live in the Midwest. The cultural Mecca for Akronites is Cleveland, about 35 miles north on the shores of Lake Erie. Some of the Broadway shows come to Cleveland, and the Metropolitan Opera comes for a week each spring. The Cleveland Orchestra is one of the finest in the country, and I go to their concerts quite often.

You are lucky to be able to attend the Shakespearean productions you mentioned. Here in America, if a girl your age expressed an interest in Shakespeare, she would be considered quite odd. Students here have no interest in the finer things in life! When you said you liked music, you were immediately placed on a pedestal far above the common herd. In high school, I knew only one girl and one boy who liked good music. The boy, Jack Dennis, is still my good friend, and together we have discovered the music of all the great composers. His candidate for "the greatest composer of all" is Hector Berlioz—mine is Wolfgang Amadeus Mozart.

My record collection has grown steadily over the past few years. I have symphonies by Beethoven, Brahms, Mozart and Haydn, and complete recordings of *Aida, Tosca, Faust, The Marriage of Figaro,* and just about all of the Gilbert and Sullivan operettas recorded.

Do you like poetry?

I have high hopes of saving enough money to come to England this fall. The most I can probably save is $1000, so if the airfare remains at $586, that would leave about $400 for my stay in England. How long could I live on that over there? By the way, I recently saw an English movie, *This Happy Breed*—you can probably tell me how authentic it was as to portraying English life.

It's a beautiful spring day here in Akron, but the "fresh air" coming in through my window brings a lot of soot with it—and the ever-present odor of the rubber factories. The white snow that winter brings never stays white for long in the Akron area!

I am enclosing a picture of yours truly. I do quite a bit of photography—developing my own film and making my own prints.

Sincerely, Paul

◆   ◆   ◆

Cecil Club, London
3rd May 1948
Dear Paul,

I expect you have been wondering why you haven't heard from me sooner, but the truth is I have been home for the weekend and missed receiving your second letter until last night when I returned. So please don't think me negligent, because all day I have been boiling over to get back and answer your letter.

I'll go straight to the subject of Thomas Wolfe, as I was able to get one of his books from the library. It is *The Web and The Rock*, and I am well in the middle of it. A British author you might like to read is Howard Spring. When I read his novel, *My Son, My Son*, I couldn't stop thinking about it for days. I don't know if John Galsworthy would appeal to you—his books are frightfully, frightfully English.

Yes, I do like poetry. My favorite poets are Rupert Brooke, Tennyson, Masefield and Shakespeare (in no order of preference). In your letter you say a girl in America is considered odd for liking Shakespeare. Over here the Bard has quite a following. In London there is a permanent repertory company called the Old Vic. (Heard of it?) The leading players are Sir Larry Olivier, Sir Ralph Richardson, Pamela Brown, and Celia Johnson. Vivien Leigh will be joining them this year. The younger generation here seems to be very fond of theatre, opera, ballet, and musical concerts, although, there are many who prefer lighter entertainment.

This Happy Breed was a very accurate portrayal of an average English family. As for English life in general, when it is boiled down, I don't suppose it is very different from the American way. At the moment the attitude of everybody is, "I couldn't care less." It's the favourite phrase of the hour and nearly everyone says it at least once a day. It makes me sick! Everyone just sits and doesn't do a thing to get out of the terrible hole we are in. I suppose a lot of the trouble is to do with the government really. The cabinet are such a weak-kneed lot, that nobody can judge what they are going to do next. If we had a strong man like Churchill, instead of Atlee, I am sure the difference would be noticeable in a week.

I'll tell you about my Club life here, I think. Cecil House was built in June 1939, by Mrs. Chesterton (sister-in-law of G.K. Chesterton) and subscribers. It wasn't used for its original purpose until 1946, for the war intervened, and the building was used by the Canadian Army. It now houses 72 girls. It's an awfully nice place, surprisingly so, I think. There's a well-equipped games room, where occasionally dances are held, and a laundry with irons at 1d. an hour. On the first floor there's a lounge with many armchairs and full-length sofas. It has a radio, nondescript, but it serves for local programmes. There's quite a nice dining room, with pictures on the wall—one of Queen Mary and the other a Madonna and Child. The bedrooms are shared by four girls, and quite attractive they are, too. Our floor, the top, is the luckiest because there are only two rooms on it, compared with a dozen or so on the other floors. We also have the advantage of the roof garden (as it is optimistically called), so we get a considerably quieter life than the rest of the girls.

Oh how I envy you your records! I am afraid I haven't many at all. I have to confine my music to concerts on the radio. I will be fortunate this year to take advantage of an institution that has been going strong for 53 years—the Henry Wood Promenade Concerts at the Royal Albert Hall. That is one feast of music we Londoners have to look forward to each year. The Albert Hall, which seats 10,000, is always crammed full and the queues stretch for miles.

I share your admiration for Mozart, and I think I like him best of all too—although I am not decided. His music makes me feel all queer inside—it has a peculiarly pathetic quality.

Thank you for the picture of yourself. I am very glad you sent it. My snaps are being developed, and I'll send you prints as soon as I can.

I like your idea of saving up to come to England, but I had better tell you, I don't think you will have enough to come by autumn. Spring, yes. The best thing you could do is stay with a family, I should think. I only wish I could invite you home, but that is impossible as we don't have a home of our own anymore. But when the time comes, you can rely on me to find you accommodation before you arrive. Most food over here is rationed, but you won't starve. Most restaurant charges are controlled by the Government and not allowed to exceed 2 shillings and threepence, which is very good. I sincerely hope I am not turning you off. Reading back, it looks very grim, but you would like it here, I'm sure. Anyway, just don't *dream* you are coming—make up your mind that you are. It's far from impossible!

Yours sincerely, Stephanie

P.S. I've heard a lot about the fabulous prizes your radio programmes give out—yachts, airplanes, cars, jobs for life in California, with a house in Beverly Hills! We have two quiz shows on the BBC, being *Have a Go* and *Double or Quits*. But the most they give away is the jackpot question, which amounts to 38 shillings and sixpence!

◆   ◆   ◆

Akron, May 6, 1948
Dear Stephanie,

How curious that you should begin reading Wolfe with *The Web & The Rock*—that was the first of his books that I read too! I have noted the books you mentioned and will let you know my opinions when I have read them.

How I envy you for being able to attend all those wonderful performances of Shakespeare in London! Over here, the New York productions of Shakespeare do not go unattended, but just try to put one on anywhere else in this country! I was surprised at the popularity of the Olivier film of *Henry V* over here, but then people just *had* to enjoy that!

Several weeks ago I saw the French film of *Beauty and The Beast*. It was in every sense a masterpiece. You get to like the beast so much that when he turns into a handsome prince you feel disappointed! Have you seen it? The other night I saw another French film—*Les Miserables*. I think it is one of the greatest motion pictures I have ever seen. The story is about an ex-convict trying to become an honest man, and it makes us wonder about the social conditions that make men criminals. Also, we have to wonder why we treat our fellow human beings the way we do—why wars, fighting, and all of the things that make life so miserable for so many?

Let's see—what else is new? Is the "new look" popular in England? It certainly is around here! I don't think it is at all becoming, and the only ones who profit by the longer skirts are the clothing manufacturers! In the event that you already have the "new look," I take back everything I said!

There has been a lot of discussion over here about reviving the draft for military service. I'm very much against it. I think it will only hasten the next war. I'm sure you know more about the horrors of war than I do—I only know what I've seen in the newsreels. Maybe sometime you would tell me about your experiences during the war—I'd love to hear.

In *This Happy Breed*, I noticed an awful lot of tea drinking. Do you people actually consume that much tea? I guess the food situation in Britain is not what it should be. Americans should be far more generous—we have more than enough of so many things, and it seems a pity we can't share with more needy people. I expect the Marshall Plan will help at least some of the countries in Europe.

One of the newest and most annoying types of radio programs here is one in which you may be telephoned during the broadcast. You have to answer by telling what you are doing at that moment or by answering a certain question. One of these programs is *Dinner Winner*, which calls at mealtime and you must not answer "Hello," but state what you are having for dinner that evening. The latest program of this type is also on at the dinner hour, and you must answer "Hello, Cinderella!" in order to win. As you can imagine, all of this becomes ridiculous, with people giving the wrong answers or saying silly things to innocent callers.

I have heard that Menotti's two short operas *The Telephone* and *The Medium* are playing in London. Do try to see them. I saw them in New York and loved them!

Must close for now. I like your name, by the way. I've never heard it before. Is it common over there? And how much of an accent do you have? I really do enjoy hearing the announcers on the BBC—I just love hearing you people talk!

Yours, Paul

◆   ◆   ◆

London, 7 May 1948
Dear Paul,

Currently playing at the Covent Garden Opera House is the *Swan Lake* ballet. I should like to see it, as it stars Britain's leading ballerina, Margot Fonteyn. I don't suppose I will get to see it, because there are so many different shows I want to see. For most live shows I go in the cheapest seats—that way I can see more than if I paid around 10s. a time.

I went to see *Oklahoma!* a couple of Saturdays ago. I preferred it to *Annie Get Your Gun*. But *Oklahoma!* had quite a few embarrassing passages and made our English audiences blush and cough a few times! I think you will like our theatres when you come.

This afternoon I took your advice and went to see Menotti's *The Telephone* and *The Medium*, and I wasn't very impressed I'm afraid. To tell you the truth, Paul, I thought they were pretty awful! The woman sitting next to me didn't increase my pleasure. First she ate some nasty looking sandwiches, making an objectionable noise in my ear. Then she was crunching boiled sweets and rattling the cellophane. Still hungry, she took out an orange and sucked on that. Heavens, she nearly drove me crazy!

This is really an "in-between" to reply to your letter about yourself and family.

I was born in the town of Redhill, in the county of Surrey, on the 18th August, 1931, and lived there until the age of six. The family was made up of Mum, Dad, my sister Sonia (3 years younger) and myself. In 1938 we moved ten miles west to Epsom, and on and off, have been living there until a couple of months ago. In 1941 we moved out for a year to the Isle of Wight, an island off the south coast that is famous for its warmth and sunshine. We went there mainly to escape the blitz, but in time we were homesick and returned to Epsom.

My dad worked for the General Post Office and volunteered to go to the Hebrides during the war to be a wireless operator. The weather there can be foul, and my dad not being used to such conditions, went for a walk along the cliff tops and was caught by the wind and waves and dragged over. That was in 1943, and he was never found.

My mother took up work in the Post Office and worked there until I was sixteen. She then took a housekeeping job for a retired General in Merstham, Surrey, and Sonia went to live with her, while I went to live at the Cecil Club.

I went to school first at the Primary, then not being bright enough at the age of eleven to win a scholarship to the Grammar School, I went to the Secondary School until I was sixteen. On leaving, I found a shorthand-typing job in London. I earn £3.15.0 a week. I am not fond of my occupation though—I do it to keep from starving. What I should like to do is travel all over the world and then go and live in the South Sea Islands, where the weather is always warm and there's no austerity (miserable word).

That's my autobiography, past, present, and future.

I hope I hear from you soon.

Yours Sincerely, Stephanie

◆   ◆   ◆

London, 12th May 1948

Dear Paul,

Your letters certainly are good for me, because some weeks ago I was always the last one up, but now that I am provided with an incentive, I am up with the lark. Our letters are all laid out for us on a table, and I can always pick out yours at a glance because of the lovely, bright green stamps.

I haven't seen either *Les Miserables* or *Beauty and the Beast*. The latter has just finished a long run and I have heard some enthusiastic reports about it too. You ask why do men fight? Why wars? I don't know, Paul, I honestly don't know. I think religion would be the way out, if people believed. I'm afraid I don't. I wish I could, but I just can't believe in God anymore—not after this war and the situation in Europe.

In answer to your question about my experiences during the war, I can say that during a good part of it, I was too young for it to make much of an impression. I have vague recollections of sitting in a cupboard underneath the stairs with a thumping heart, listening to the screech of falling bombs. That was in the blitz of 1940. In 1944 the flying bombs and V-2s made their appearance. I was 12 or 13 then, so can remember it all clearly. We would sit for hours in the school shelters, with our little tins of iron rations, and listen to those awful things, which had an indescribable grinding sound, utterly unlike normal aircraft. Then they would stop, seeming right overhead, and we all would sit breathless, waiting for the crash as the awful thing fell to earth. After that, the whole school was evacuated, and I went to Cornwall. I didn't fare too badly during the war—the worst thing of course was the loss of my dad.

I did laugh when you asked how much of an accent I have. Well, I can't describe it for you, I'm afraid. Just the King's English I suppose. Not Cockney, not Lancashire, Yorkshire, Welsh, or Cornish, but plain southeast England. What sort of an accent have you?

It's taking the "New Look" quite a time to become popular here, as everyone is so conservative about dress. I can understand your scorn of it. How could a mere man think otherwise? After all, he has been wearing the same old outfit for nigh on a hundred years. But with a woman, it's different—she must wear something different or her morale is affected. Anyway, the "look" *is* becoming—far more feminine!

This Happy Breed was very truthful about tea drinking. The English really do drink that amount—even more. They have it brought to them in bed in the morning, two cups for breakfast, one at elevenses, one after lunch, two for tea in the afternoon, and sometimes for supper—but more often cocoa. Of course if a crisis occurs during the day, a cup of tea must be consumed on the strength of the great comfort it is supposed to give. I must be an oddity, because I hate the stuff!

Maybe the food situation in Britain isn't what it should be, but I'm not going to complain about it. Compared to other countries in Europe, we really do eat well. The butter ration is three ounces a week, sugar three pounds a month, cheese one ounce a week, two ounces of bacon a week, and one egg a fortnight.

I'm glad you like my name. It isn't at all common over here—I've never known another Stephanie.

Ta Ta For Now, Stephanie

◆   ◆   ◆

Akron, May 12, 1948
Dear Stephanie,

I looked up the exchange rate for British money and learned that a pound is worth $4.03, and a shilling is worth 20 cents in our money. But your monetary system still seems highly confusing to me. Can you give me a breakdown? Particularly, tell me what the signs stand for.

Your comments on the Promenade Concerts make them sound enjoyable. It seems you British use the term "Promenade" for concerts of light music. It took me a long time to figure out what they were talking about on the BBC when they referred to the "Boston Promenade Orchestra." I finally deduced they meant the "Boston Pops." I suppose "Pops" is too unsophisticated for the British.

I'm always interested in hearing about the plays, concerts, etc. that you attend. I too buy cheap seats so that I can see more things. If ten shillings is $2.00 in our money, that doesn't seem like much for the better seats. For concerts here, you pay anywhere from $1 to $10. In Akron, the first-run movie theatres charge about 75 cents, and the second-run theatres charge 35 cents.

I was glad to hear about your family, your life up to now, and your plans for the future. If you are only earning a little over 3 pounds a week at present, that doesn't seem like very much money for such a job. I think you had better leave England if you intend to accumulate any kind of fortune at all! If I translate my earnings into pounds, I guess I make about 12 pounds a week. My dad is the foreman of he bricklayers, and he collects something like 25 pounds a week.

I'm glad you like poetry. I share your admiration for Rupert Brooke—I first encountered him in Richard Halliburton's book, *The Glorious Adventure*. Halliburton visited Brooke's grave "on some corner of a foreign field." I discovered Tennyson in Halliburton too. I especially love the poem entitled *Ulysses*:

> For always roaming with a hungry heart,
> Much have I seen and known—cities of men
> And manners, climates, councils, governments,
> Myself not least, but honored of them all…

Are you withstanding my barrage of letters all right? I do want them to please you, so let me know if there is anything special you want to hear.

We are having summer weather here at the moment—above 80 degrees the past few days.

So long for now, Paul

◆   ◆   ◆

Akron, May 15, 1948
Dear Stephanie,

This past week I was put to work with a shovel and wheelbarrow, hauling dirt to fill in around the foundation of a new building. Every night I came home with arms and back aching, blisters on my hands, and just feeling generally wretched! On top of everything else, I got a nasty sunburn! Oh well, we get a raise next week—it amounts to about a pound and a half more per week.

I have been doing some reading this weekend. Thanks a million for recommending *My Son, My Son* by Howard Spring. I read a good half of it last night and finished it off this morning. Like you, I will not be able to forget the book for a long time. I finally finished *The Forsyte Saga* the other day, but it was quite a struggle. I just couldn't get interested—maybe because, as you said, the characters are so "frightfully, frightfully English."

Another book I read recently is *The Gallery* by John Horne Burns. The setting is in Naples during the Second World War; it is not a pretty sort of story, but it serves the same purpose as *All Quiet on The Western Front*—an anti-war novel.

Sorry you didn't like *The Medium* and *The Telephone*. I didn't mean to give you a bum steer—I really thought you would like them. And the lady sitting next to you! Is there nothing one is *not* permitted to do in your theatres?

There is an article in the current *Harper's* magazine called, "How They Fly the Atlantic." As you can imagine, I found it most interesting.

If it's a nice day tomorrow, I might persuade Dad to go for a drive. We have a brand new 1948 Mercury car—really super! I can't drive it alone yet—I am still in the process of learning.

Sincerely yours, Paul

◆   ◆   ◆

London, 22 May 1948
Dear Paul,

I went to the Travel Association the other day and they said you would manage very well on $400 for a month's stay. At the moment there are many different coach tours to all parts of the country. I think you are going to like our countryside and villages, because they really are beautiful. The Travel Association gave me a couple of illustrated booklets, which I am sending under separate cover.

I had a wonderful time this morning. I went up to Oxford Street to find myself a new dress. As I told you, it had to be the "New Look," and eventually I found something I liked. It's a striped one, in navy blue and white, with a three-quarter-length skirt (drawing enclosed). Oh dear, I hope I'm not boring you with all this!

Thomas Wolfe and I are coming along quite well. About those love scenes though, I have never read anything quite like it before. I can't fathom why he had to include every little detail. I consider that kind of thing private, and consequently find his descriptions quite nauseating!

Yes, I am withstanding your "barrage of letters" O.K. I love receiving them and only wish I could make mine as interesting.

When you said your Dad earns 25 pounds a week, I nearly passed out! Over here his job would bring in about 10 pounds per week, and yours about 5 pounds. Your cost of living must be much, much higher than ours.

As to our money system, here are the signs, not that there are many of them: £ = pound, s. = shilling, and d. = pence. These are our coins and notes: farthing (1/4 penny), halfpenny, penny, threepence, sixpence, shilling, florin (2 shillings), half crown (2 shillings and sixpence), crown (5 shillings, but practically extinct), 10s. note, one pound note, and 5 pound note. (Notes are bills in your language.) Is that any help?

I was sorry to learn of your aches and pains from your work, but I hope you are better now. I suppose all this work will make you a strong, Tarzan-like creature by the end of the summer. Do you think so?

It must have been my way of putting it, but you got me rather wrong about the Promenade Concerts. They happen every year and are the most famous of all our musical festivals. It is the peak of a musician's fame to get into the Promenade Concerts. The word "Promenade" is used because there is a section of the Albert Hall going under that name. Why we call your Boston "Pops" Orchestra is because it plays a type of music heard at the seaside in summer on the Promenade. I hope I have made myself clear to you because, reading it through, the paragraph looks somewhat confused!

What a funny phrase to use, "bum steer." The first word has an entirely different meaning over here, I'm sure.

Hope I hear from you again soon, Stephanie

◆   ◆   ◆

Akron, May 27, 1948
Dear Stephanie,

Everybody here is rejoicing. We have a new gas oven and range—the latest model! Mom has celebrated by making some apple and pumpkin pies today, and I can hardly wait to get into them!

I must take some pictures of Akron teen-age girls to send to you. The high school girls around here are running around looking like hillbillies. They wear men's overall trousers (called "jeans") and men's white shirts with the shirttails hanging out and fluttering in the breeze. What a mess! Then too, there is an excessive use of makeup—or at least I think so. In my opinion (as a mere man), it is a shame to cover up a young girl's natural beauty—her lips are already a beautiful color, and her cheeks are rosy enough. I can hear you calling me all sorts of names, so I think I had better drop the subject!

Had a letter from you today—also a packet of magazines. Thanks for the photographs you took in Surrey, and for the travel booklets about Britain you are sending. You are really getting me excited about coming to England.

It seemed perfectly natural for me to ask about your accent, but now when you ask me the same question, I have to laugh too! I don't know how to describe mine—I don't talk as you do, that's for certain!

I am making preparations for a Memorial Day weekend visit to Pennsylvania with my dad. The town we are going to visit is about 200 miles from here—right in the center of the state.

Today was payday! I wish the government didn't take so much of my money. After income tax and social security, I only get $50.60 out of $58.00. We have an Englishman bricklayer at work, named Freddy. He has been in the U.S. for many years, but still has quite an accent. Today he told me a story about twelve New York policemen who were sent to London to learn how they direct traffic over there. It seems that six of them died of pneumonia, and the other six got run over!

Sincerely, Paul

◆   ◆   ◆

London, 2nd June 1948
Dear Paul,

After half an hour's washing of my "smalls," I can sit down for an hour to write to you.

I found a good map today and shall send it with some magazines I have put by for you. Thanks a lot for the magazines and theatre programmes, which arrived today along with two letters from you.

I liked hearing your opinion of girls' makeup, but I don't see how you can say every girl has a beautiful color, though. I think it varies. I don't like to see a lot of heavy makeup, but I do use some—a small amount of cream, powder and lipstick. I don't touch rouge, varnish, mascara or any horrors of that sort.

I've read about your high school girls wearing the sort of things you mentioned, but do they actually wear them to school? If I appeared in anything like your girls wear, I wouldn't be able to show my face in the street. People would think I was mad! Isn't it funny how we people who are so much alike in so many ways, can differ so much in others?

Your Englishman acquaintance interests me exceedingly. I love the story about the policemen—it *was* funny. Give him my best wishes.

I went out for a walk yesterday and was wondering if you would enjoy walking through our countryside. Do Americans walk much? I have read that walking isn't at all popular in your country—that you use the car for practically every journey, long or short. We use bikes a lot over here, but I prefer to walk.

I lost my sweet ration coupons last month, so was unable to have any sweets (candy) then. This month we were allowed 12 ounces and I spent my ration all on Kit-Kat, a form of chocolate wafer biscuit. That's about my favorite—what's yours?

Shall I tell you—shall I? Oh, I might as well! I've got my hair cut in a fringe! Does that startle you? I like it myself.

'Til I hear from you again, Stephanie

♦   ♦   ♦

Akron, June 2, 1948
Dear Stephanie,

I brought back a few pieces of hotel stationery to write you this letter about our trip to Pennsylvania.

Dad, Grandpa and I left Akron at 5:00 AM Saturday, but didn't get to Philipsburg until late in the day because we stopped to visit relatives in three other Pennsylvania towns. Philipsburg is the small town to which my great grandfather came from Liverpool in the late 1860's. My grandfather was born in England, but was only a baby when the family emigrated. My dad was born in Philipsburg, and he thinks this is "God's Country." It *is* beautiful, and I took lots of photographs.

On Sunday morning we went to the cemetery, high on a hill overlooking the town, to watch the Memorial Day ceremonies. They had the usual parade with the high school band, army veterans, boy scouts, etc. After the speeches at the cemetery, the American Legion soldiers fired guns in salute to the men who died in America's wars. While Dad and Grandpa talked with relatives and friends, I stretched out on the hillside where I had a view of the cemetery and the town below. I wished I could speak to all those people buried on the mountain-side—the builders, the drunkards, the church-going men and women, the good and the bad—all now being honored and remembered on Memorial Day.

Later, we went to the Old Cemetery in town, where my Grandpa's mother is buried. There's no marker or anything, but I took a picture of Grandpa pointing to the site of the grave.

I kept wishing you were along so I could show things to you. Along the high-ways we have a number of Burma Shave signs—about 8 or 10 in a row, each containing a few words of a jingle. One of my favorites is: "A man/a miss/a car/a curve./He kissed/the miss/and missed/the curve!"

Well, I'm off to the darkroom to do my photographs.

Sincerely, Paul

◆   ◆   ◆

London, 6th June 1948
Dear Paul,

Thank you for your letter written on the hotel notepaper. You made your trip sound very enviable, and I certainly would have liked to come too. I'm sure I like travelling as much as you do, and to be bowling along in a car over miles of American road would be wizard. Perhaps in five years' time I'll be able to do that. It will be fine though, if you come to England next spring—it will give me the opportunity to see some of our famous beauty spots, that is if you want anyone to go around with you. Some people prefer their own company when visiting.

I went to the Derby yesterday, but had no luck at all. There were easily 100,000 people there, and all the usual tipsters, bookies, gypsies, cockle and whelk stalls, fairs, and hellfire preachers shouting the wrath of God is forever upon us, and we'll all go to the burning pit! In the grandstand, gray top hats were almost uniform, and the women had the most wonderful dresses—all New Look!

A couple of snaps are enclosed. They aren't very good, especially as they make me appear far too large around the waist. That's on account of having no belt on my frock.

Bye for now, Stephanie

♦   ♦   ♦

Akron, June 10, 1948
Dear Stephanie,

Today I received a wonderful letter from you, enclosing two photos. I certainly do thank you for sending them! I think your hair looks extra super the way you have it, and I recognize the material of the dress from the sample you sent. You look very nice in your "new look"—I must admit!

I enjoyed your tale of the Derby. Perhaps I will be there to go with you next year? Anyway, when I do come to England, I hope you will go with me everywhere I visit.

By the way, I have been meaning to ask you—do you like opera very much? I hope so, because you're going to see some when I come, if I have to drag you there with a rope!

Sincerely, Paul

♦   ♦   ♦

London, 14th June 1948
Dear Paul,

How can I thank you enough for the New York photographs, which arrived today? Everyone in my room is in raptures over them! How did you manage to take the one looking down on Liberty's book? And the wonderful pictures of the skyscrapers! I'm still laughing at the picture of your friend in his pajamas—fast asleep! The one called "Looking down from the Empire State Building" just took my breath away—how different New York is from London!

I also received letter #30 and the bundle of magazines, so you see I have had a wonderful time reading all of them. I don't think there is a magazine in the world to beat *Life*. The article on sex education interested me a lot. It seems the wisest way of going about it—to learn "the facts of life" (stupid phrase) from the cradle. Such a lot of trouble is caused through ignorance. I was never told anything, except what I heard from the girls at school when I was about eleven. Until then my idea was that doctors brought the babies in little black bags. I have never understood why we are kept in ignorance for so long—it's dammed stupid, really. Anyway, what are your views?

I'll be glad to go down to Merstham this weekend—it will be cooler and so quiet after London's heat and continuous roar. In Merstham, when I wake up in the morning, all I can hear is the cuckoo and other birds singing—it's wonderful!

There's no need to drag me by rope to see operas when you come—I'll go quite quietly. Where shall it be? Covent Garden?

Good night! Stephanie

◆   ◆   ◆

Akron, June 18, 1948
Dear Stephanie,

I was happy to hear the New York pictures finally arrived. I took the photo of Liberty's tablet from one of the square holes in her crown—you have to climb stairs and stairs and stairs to get there! Anyway, I'm glad you enjoyed the pictures.

I knew you would like *Life* magazine, and I shall send it to you regularly. As for the article on sex education, very few schools over here have such courses. At Central High we had some sex education in our biology classes. Over about a two-week period, we had movies, slides, lectures and opportunities to ask questions. The biology classes are separate for boys and girls, but even so, most of us were rather shy about asking questions. In the end we were asked to write our questions and put them in a box! Anyway, at that age, I don't think we learned much that we didn't already know.

Last Sunday, Dennis and I went for a walk through Perkins' Woods, a park near the center of Akron. In the park is a memorial to John Brown. Do you know your American history enough to know who he was? At one time he lived in Akron, and his former home is now a museum. Brown was a famous emancipator of slaves, and he was finally hanged after he led a raid at Harper's Ferry.

My savings have now reached the $100 mark. I told Dennis of my plan to visit England, and he envies me I'm sure. When I showed him your picture, he said he would go too if he were me! I think you look very pretty in those pictures, so don't be sorry you sent them!

It looks as if the draft bill is going to pass in congress and the president will certainly sign it. I feel miserable! I might not even be able to make my trip to England next spring—oh despair! Write some words of consolation if you can.

Meantime, I must now take my turn to travel to the land of Nod...

Yours, Paul

◆   ◆   ◆

London, 21ˢᵗ June 1948
Dear Paul,

Or perhaps I should say "Poor Paul," because you have all my sympathy in regard to that miserable Draft bill. You aren't going to let this put you off though, surely. If the conscription doesn't start until early next year, why don't you come here at Christmastime? Otherwise you'll be in the army for two years, and goodness knows what will happen in that time. Why we'll be old then! Our whole outlook on life will have changed.

The next thing for me to do is thank you for the photographs I received on Friday. It's nice to see what Akron looks like and some of the Ohio countryside.

Oddly enough, I have heard of your Mr. John Brown! In fact, when I was about nine years old I saw a film about him and was very impressed. I use to think about him for weeks after, and how unjustly he was treated.

T.T.F.N., Stephanie

◆   ◆   ◆

Akron, June 25, 1948
Dear Stephanie,

"Poor Paul" isn't the expression to use now. I no longer have to worry about being drafted! Before President Truman signed the bill into law, I enlisted in the Ohio National Guard. I had to enlist for 3 years, but I have only to drill for two hours a week and go to camp for two weeks each summer. So that means I can still come to England next spring as planned!

I was feeling low for a time though, and I thought about your idea of moving to a South Sea Island to escape all this madness. I don't think it would work though—you can't go back to a less-civilized state.

Dennis and I went to see the French film *Children of Paradise. Life* magazine called it the French answer to *Gone With The Wind*—and what an answer it is! Hollywood could never do anything like it! It's rather a sad sort of film that seems to portray the futility of human life. The "children of paradise" are all of us, and when we view ourselves honestly we laugh at first, then are moved to pity. I do hope you get to see it!

Sincerely, Paul

◆   ◆   ◆

London, 30th June 1948
Dear Paul,

You were pretty sharp to get into the National Guard.

Well, we are back to where we started now—you are coming in the spring. At the moment I can see quite a few Americans in London. They are easy to pick out, mainly because of their clothing.

So you don't think a desert isle would work out? Well, of course it would have to be perfect: a wonderful house, a blue lagoon (no sharks), banana trees, a couple of cows, sun all the time, and plenty of local food. And then I should be satisfied! Oh no—I would need yards and yards of material to have lots of clothes!

Gertrude and I have been feeling so "choc-a-flipping block" that we felt we must have some cream cakes and coffee to cheer us up. So, that we have done, and I have returned to finish this letter.

I have had a bumper mail from you this past week, including packages of magazines with *Life, New Yorker, Omnibook, Seventeen,* and *Opera News.* Thanks a lot. I just love the ads in your magazines. Ours have a more take-it-or-leave-it attitude—yours are much more persuasive. Instance: "Heads turn…hearts yearn…for the keen teen with the new fashion plate complexion." It's all very lovely and soothing to read, I find.

Yours sincerely, Stephanie

◆ ◆ ◆

Akron, July 5, 1948
Dear Stephanie,

Enclosed you will find a couple of pictures of me—as good as can be done, I guess, considering the subject matter! Do I look American? That is a yellow T-shirt I am wearing!

If you had the island you describe, I think I'd be pleading to go with you. But you'd have to add one thing—a record player and lots of Mozart recordings!

As you have probably heard, Dewey received the Republican nomination for president. I had a great time listening to the convention when it was on the radio—I stayed up until 3:00 AM one night, listening to the speeches and demonstrations.

I have been meaning to tell you about James Joyce and his famous book *Ulysses*. It describes in exhaustive detail, the mental and physical wanderings during a single day of the life of the hero, Stephen Dedalus. Actually, you are interloping on the minds of three people, and since the mind doesn't think in punctuated sentences, the book doesn't make for easy reading! I'm afraid Joyce wrote his books mostly to please himself—his last book, *Finnegan's Wake*, is almost impossible to understand and they might just as well have buried the book with him!

Yours, Paul

◆ ◆ ◆

London, 9th July 1948
Dear Paul,

Thanks for your latest letter and a packet of magazines.

I quite enjoyed the article in *Atlantic* by James Hilton about the English boy who stayed in America during the war. Evidently, the point of the tale was that if the boy had continued living in your country, he would have had a much happier time than he did when returning to England and his old school. And I can quite believe it. I am inclined to think that American children have a far more enjoyable time than their English equivalents. I think I would like to live in America, and am quite sure I would be happy there too. I can't say England needs me, because we have far too many people here already. The country would right itself far more quickly if a few ten thousand folk would emigrate. The trouble with us is that we just live on tradition. That's why we are about twenty or thirty years behind America in progress.

This week is the starting of our new National Health Service. Mr. Atlee spoke over the radio the other night, giving it a proper introduction. It really is a very good thing for our country, although the amount of insurance that comes out of our wages each week from now on is quite alarming. It is in the region of 5 shillings (about $1), but still—no more doctors' bills, no hospital bills, free dentures, free spectacles—even free glass eyes! Here's to the success of the new scheme and every success as well!

I haven't decided whether or not I shall be alone on my island. I should be very bored with my own company, I know. Your idea of a gramophone with Mozart recordings brings to mind a radio show we have here called *Desert Island Discs*. Each week some famous person selects the eight recordings he would choose if he was cast on a desert island with a gramophone and an endless supply of needles.

Sometimes when I read your letters, I try to imagine you saying the words in your American accent. I haven't much idea of how you speak, although I suppose it is something like an average person in an American film. Thank you for sending the snaps—I like them very much. You certainly *do* look *very* American. So that is a T-shirt you have on! There was an article in *Life* about them, which interested me a lot. They seem such an asset—I wish I had one! Nothing like that is on sale here.

Nite-nite, Stephanie

◆   ◆   ◆

Akron, July 14, 1948
Dear Stephanie,

Finally, I have an evening to spend with you. I have so little time of my own these days—mostly because of the Guard. We had to camp out all of last weekend, and it wasn't much fun. Anyway, please don't think me mean or negligent for not writing as often these days.

Sad news! Akron simply cannot support anything of cultural value! The Liberty Theatre has discontinued showing foreign films—otherwise, they say, they would go broke! I guess I'll have to go to Cleveland now to see anything any good.

I have learned that a vacation is a legitimate excuse from Guard drills, so that means I can take time off for England next spring without any trouble. I expect I will be able to stay for a month when I come. As to what all I would like to see and do, I think I would like you to be my travel agent—you can plan my whole trip, and you can begin right now by suggesting the best time to come in the spring. I do hope we like each other a lot when we meet, and I hope we can do a lot of things together.

'Til next time, Paul

◆   ◆   ◆

London, 20th July 1948
Dear Paul,

Of course I forgive you for not writing. Anyway, you have a substantial excuse, and I can't say the same for myself. It's me who should be asking forgiveness, not you!

Yes, I think I should like to be your travel agent. As regards the best time to come, I should think April would be best—"Oh to be in England, now that April's there!" It certainly will be a lot of fun making plans. What a long time it does seem to wait though.

There's nothing outstanding to tell you, I fear. Yesterday I went to see *Fantasia*. I adored it and could see it again and again! Some time next week I hope to see *Fort Apache*, with Henry Fonda, Shirley Temple and John Wayne. It's a rip-roarin' tale of the frontier, so I think I shall like it a lot. I am really fond of a good western.

Today I was actually subject to a London bus conductor's good manners. They are normally the rudest people who inhabit the earth, but today when I asked one to change a ten-shilling note, he did so with a smile!

Hope to hear from you again soon.

Stephanie

◆   ◆   ◆

Akron, July 24, 1948
Dear Stephanie,

I am listening to *Music in Miniature* on the BBC at the moment—it is mostly chamber music, with a few songs thrown in now and then.

I have just put another $70 in the bank, bringing my fund up to $250. This requires a lot of scrimping and scraping, but I am determined to save $1000 by the end of January.

I have been reading a book about Hart Crane and find it very interesting. Crane was an American poet who lived much of his life in Ohio, the state of his birth. As a matter of fact, he lived in Akron for a time, and he wrote a poem on the subject:

> GREETING the dawn
> A shift of rubber workers presses down
> South Main…
> Akron, "high place"—
> A bunch of smoking hills
> Among the rolling hills.

He goes on to mention the many immigrants who have come to Akron to work in the factories. (We do have a lot of them still—also people from the hills of West Virginia and Tennessee.) Akron has changed somewhat since Crane lived here, but there is still very little available of cultural value.

You want to know what I intend to do after I come to England. I wish I could tell you—I honestly do. I don't suppose I will continue laboring for long, although I sometimes think I'd rather earn my bread by the sweat of my brow instead of by having some kind of white-collar job. It's sort of hard to explain my feelings about all this.

You and your Westerns! *Fort Apache* is currently playing in Akron and I *might* go to see it. But I doubt it!

Good night, Paul

◆   ◆   ◆

Merstham, 1ˢᵗ August 1948
Dear Paul,

How can I thank you for those beautiful books I received yesterday!—*Fair is Our Land* and *Ever New England.* The pictures have such an effect on me, I feel I must take the next boat across the Atlantic to see such a heavenly land as yours. Thank you very much for them—they are something I will always prize.

I have been reading a most interesting book, *Weeping Wood,* by Vicki Baum. It's all about rubber and there are quite a few chapters devoted to Akron. It describes the overpowering smell of rubber from the factories and the unfinished, dirty appearance of a town that "had grown so fast she hadn't caught up with herself." A number of places are mentioned: Goodyear Heights, Firestone Park, Akron University, Mayflower Hotel and even the Armory!

I am home for the August Bank Holiday weekend. There is a wonderful crop of lavender growing here in the garden, and I have been picking some to dry in the sun. It's my intention to make some lavender bags and take them back to London.

I have heard something of the strictness of the town of Boston, but I think they have now surpassed themselves in trying to censor Olivier's film of *Hamlet.* Heavens above, as only Shakespeare enthusiasts will see the film anyway, what good will their removing certain passages be?

Sincerely, Stephanie

◆   ◆   ◆

Akron, August 8, 1948
Dear Stephanie,

Last night Dennis and I went to see *The Time of Your Life,* with James Cagney. It was a different kind of role for Cagney, but he played it very well. Roughly, the action of the film may be described as a day at Nick's Joint, where Joe (Cagney) hangs out. Joe loves everybody, and his hobby is making people happy. I hope you get to see it—I recommend it highly.

The film was playing at Loew's, probably the best of our downtown theatres. It is elaborately decorated as a sort of Moorish palace, with all kinds of statuary scattered throughout the building. Probably the most original thing is the ceiling. When you look up, you see clouds (actually drifting by) and stars all over the place. Do you have anything like that in any of your theatres?

Thanks for sending those reviews of American films. The comments on *The World & His Wife* (called *State of the Nation* over here) amused me a great deal. I fear that Milton Schulman came closer to the truth than he realized when he said, "In fact, one would gather from this film that the average American voter has the political maturity of a new-laid egg."

Well, next week I am off to camp! I will be writing you from there, but you should continue to send your letters here. We are going to Camp Atterbury, near Indianapolis, Indiana—you should be able to find it on a map.

To get around to more pleasant subjects, a number of Broadway plays will be coming to Cleveland this fall, including *Man & Superman,* and a new play by Tennessee Williams.

At the moment I am in the middle of a book called *Winesburg, Ohio,* by Sherwood Anderson. It is a collection of short stories and sketches of small town life in Ohio. Another recent book acquisition is *The Journey Down* by Aline Bernstein—the real-life Esther of Wolfe's *Web & The Rock.* Mrs. Bernstein wrote the same love story from her point of view, and it is supposed to be very good. My copy is a signed first edition, and it only cost me $1.50!

Have you heard the news that Hollywood has done a film of *Carmen* with Rita Hayworth in the title role? Can you imagine Miss Hayworth in lavish, colorful clothes, with every hair in place, playing the dirty, common little prostitute? Oh well…

Until next time, Paul

◆   ◆   ◆

Camp Atterbury, Indiana, August 16, 1948
Dear Stephanie,

The first day of camp is now over. The only trouble is we have twelve more to go!

What lousy food they dish out! Everyone is complaining about it, and we hope it will improve soon.

Well, this is just the briefest note to let you know that all is well—more or less—and I'll write more soon.

Sincerely, Paul

◆   ◆   ◆

London, 17th August 1948
Dear Paul,

You are away at camp as I write this letter and I hope you are faring well.

First of all, thank you for the copy of *Look Homeward, Angel* that has now reached me safely. You know, you are too good to me, because I have also received a couple of *Life* magazines and the package of New York newspapers.

In one of the papers I noticed a strip cartoon—*Steve Canyon* by Milton Canniff. About a year ago, our *Daily Express* carried it for a while, but it received so many complaints from readers, who said that the paper was becoming a glorified "Comic Cuts," that in the end they stopped printing it. But other papers include strip cartoons. *The London Daily Mirror* has a shocking young woman named Jane, whose clothes are conspicuous by their absence. She was very popular with the services during the war and quite believably helped to keep up their morale.

During the next week I will be sending you some hotel brochures and other information for your visit to Britain, with prices worked out in dollars (I hope!). From now on, I will be noting down different things you must be sure to see when you are here.

I'm afraid I don't like the sound of *The Time of Your Life*. I am terribly fond of James Cagney, but I don't think I'd like to see him in that sentimental kind of part. I like my Cagney tough, I'm afraid. Your Loew's Theatre sounds marvelous—there is no cinema of that sort here—not with clouds drifting by and stars!

Last Saturday morning I went with a friend to see the closing ceremony of the Olympic Games. The whole show lasted about 6 hours—four of them were taken up with Les Prix des Nations, an equestrian event with 44 competitors from nine nations. When that part of the programme was finished, flags of every nation were carried out into the arena by boy scouts, and the Olympic flag was presented to the Lord Mayor of London for safe keeping until 1952, when Finland will take it over. *Non Noblis Domine* was sung by massed choirs conducted by Malcom Sargeant, while the flame slowly went out. Then the whole 82,000 people in the stadium joined in singing a special cantata written by A.P. Herbert to the tune of *Londonderry Air*. The whole ceremony was somehow very moving, and afterwards, my friend and I both agreed that we had lumps in our throats.

Last Sunday morning, I went with some of the girls to Petticoat Lane Market in the East End. The market is an area of some four streets—all crammed full of stalls and barrows, and selling practically everything. The object of our visit was to search for nylons, because Petticoat Lane is just about the only place they can be found. I bought a pair of lovely sheer blue ones. We stopped at one stocking stall where a man was practically giving his away—ordinary rayon stockings at four pairs for five shillings ($1.00). For all that, nobody would buy them, and the man got quite mad. "Cor, strike me pink," he said, "You're a greedy lot of geezers! Come on, they're all stolen property—I pinched the lot myself!" Which was no doubt true. These people are quite open about it—except when a policeman comes their way!

When you come I expect you will enjoy looking round for bargains at the second-hand bookshops in Charing Cross Road. Are new books expensive in America? Nothing can be purchased here for under 15 s. ($3.00).

Cheerio for now, Stephanie

◆   ◆   ◆

Akron, August 31, 1948
Dear Stephanie,

Let me get down on my knees and beg forgiveness! I mean for not writing for two weeks! While I was at camp I had such a very little time of my own that I decided to use it for picture taking and sightseeing, and then write lots to you when I got home. And so here I am, back home again after two weeks under the blazing Indiana sun.

Oh God, I really am frustrated! I've got so much to tell you and so many things to catch up on. I have all the magazines and letters you sent while I was away, and lots of darkroom work to do, and—oh dear!

Will you excuse me for tonight? I promise—and I really mean it—to make up for the last two weeks during the next two!

Yours, Paul

◆   ◆   ◆

London 3rd September 1948
Dear Paul,

When I went down to breakfast this morning, I thought to myself, if I don't hear from Paul today, it's very doubtful whether I shall hear from him again. But somehow the fates determined that I should receive a letter. You know, I really thought something serious had happened—that somebody at camp had mistaken you for a practice target—yes, that you had been killed, for those things do happen.

I also wondered if you had grown weary of writing so many letters to me, and felt you couldn't write any more for a while. If that's so, please tell me, because the situation could probably be remedied. The correspondence could be dropped for a couple of months and then picked up again at a later date. Don't think I'm saying that because I'm bored, because that's far from the truth—I am always eager to receive each letter from you.

On its way to you at the moment is a copy of Paul Gallico's *The Snow Goose*. It really is a haunting little tale and is beautifully written.

Yesterday and the day before, I have been in bed with a cold—yes, right in the middle of all this heat! But don't pity me—I read books and had lots of sleep, and in fact was sorry to get better!

Today is the 9th anniversary of Britain's declaration of war upon Germany. Nearly a decade has passed! It makes me feel sort of desolate when I think about it.

We took some snaps on the roof the other day. One came out well enough to send to you, and that I'll do in a week's time.

Yours, Stephanie

◆   ◆   ◆

Akron, September 5, 1948
Dear Stephanie,

This will be the account I promised you of my two weeks at Camp Atterbury.

When we arrived that first evening, we had time only to make our cots and "hit the sack." We had to get up at 4:30 AM, and after washing, dressing, and making our cots, we had to "police up" (pick up all the bits of paper and trash around the barracks) before breakfast, which was served at 6:00. After that we had to sweep, mop, and generally clean up the inside of the barracks.

For the first week we spent most of our time training. Supper was at 6:00 PM, and the evenings were free. I spent my evenings walking around the camp. Actually, the part we were using was only a wee small corner of the place—there are hundreds and hundreds of buildings stretching for miles. It's hard to explain how one feels looking at these abandoned buildings—thousands of men passed through here during the war, and many of them never made it back home.

On Saturday I got a pass to go into a nearby, small, jerk-water town near the camp. Most of the fellows headed straight for the beer joints, but I found another guy who wasn't interested in drinking. We visited the local library and then settled on a bench in the public square to talk about books, philosophy, etc. Later on, we joined up with another soldier and shared a taxi back to camp. It only cost $1.00 apiece, and it was quicker than the bus.

We were allowed to sleep in on Sunday morning, and at 11:00 AM, passes were again available. This time I got to go to Indianapolis. My three companions were all out to find themselves "a skirt," so I went my own way after we arrived in town. I spent the afternoon looking over the city and ended up going to a movie I wanted to see again—*The Time of Your Life!*

After the show, I walked around the Soldiers and Sailors Monument for a time—it really is beautiful when they light it up at night! It is located in the center of town, with a traffic circle around it, and the streets run out in all directions like the spokes of a wheel. As the evening wore on, I sat on a thick stone railing by a fountain, watching the pigeons cluster on the top of the monument and the soldiers cluster around the base. I finally got back to camp at around 1:00 AM.

The second week was more irregular than the first. We had gas mask drill, instructions on using the compass, etc. What I found hard to take was bayonet practice. They made us scream, yell, and make all kinds of animalistic noises—trying to bring out the beast in us. I know of at least one soldier who did not have his heart in that sort of thing!

On Friday, I volunteered for overnight guard duty on one of the railway cars that contained our equipment. I'm afraid I didn't do very well. I fell asleep at about 3:00 AM, and didn't wake up until 6:00!

Saturday was our last day at camp, so the officers decided to sponsor a beer party in the barracks. A sad mistake, as it turned out, because it soon turned into a drunken brawl with several guys all cut up and badly hurt. They were going after each other with bayonets! No one got any sleep that night, and we all had to help clean up the mess in the barracks.

We left on Sunday and arrived back in Akron about 3:00 AM Monday morning. So now you have some idea of what it is like at "Summer Camp."

Bye for now, Paul

◆   ◆   ◆

Akron, September 8, 1948
Dear Stephanie,

Dear, dear, dear, dear Stephanie! I have just received your letter in which you suggest that maybe I am tired of writing to you. I hope that day never comes! Really and truly, don't ever let your mind entertain such thoughts again! The reason I didn't write more from camp was simply that free time was so precious, and I was usually dead tired at the end of the day. Even here at home, the days just don't have enough hours in them. But my heart's in the right place—I *want* to write a lot more than I do!

Thank you for the book you are sending. I think I shall enjoy it very much.

At last I have finished my pictures taken at camp. I have made some enlargements, which I plan to take to the armory and sell to the guys.

I now have $350 deposited in my bank account. I still expect to reach my goal of $1000 by the end of January.

After reading enthusiastic reviews, I just had to buy Aldous Huxley's new book, *Ape & Essence*. It describes what the world will be like in the 22nd century, after the Third World War. The devil is in command! All through the book, Huxley stresses the point that people knew what they were heading for—swearing they would change direction—but kept on doing things that sent them farther along the road to damnation. I think Mr. Huxley is absolutely right about this. What we gain for our individual countries by excessive nationalism, we lose in the long run, because we've taken it from the rest of the world.

Sincerely, Paul

◆   ◆   ◆

Akron, September 12, 1948
Dear Stephanie,

My brother Ted arrived home from Italy yesterday, and I have been up to my ears in doing his film processing. He really did take some swell pictures! He has been telling us of his adventures, and one of them was rather scary. He and another American were chased along the street in Rome by a band of Reds, and they had to take refuge in a small café. The owner of the place locked the door and kept them safe until the mob dispersed. Italy doesn't seem like the ideal place to visit right now.

All the talk of war has led me to wonder if we'll ever get to see each other. I can't believe there will be another war before next year, but all those headlines keep staring you in the face!

As per usual, I have lots of things I should be writing about, but I feel sort of dreamy tonight. "I, a stranger and afraid, in a world I never made." A.E. Housman wrote those lines, and that's about how I feel at the moment. The blackness of the night is all around me, the crickets are chirping, and occasionally I hear a car going by on Hazel Street. It's a Sunday night in September, and I sit and wonder what I'm doing here and what I'll do with the rest of my life. Most of all I lack security: I have no religion, no firm convictions about life, and I have no one to love or to love me. The night closes in around me and I think about these things, knowing that in the morning I will go about my daily routine as unconcerned as ever.

But tonight, I'm lonely.

Good night, Paul

◆   ◆   ◆

Gillingham, 12th September 1948
Dear Paul,

I certainly did enjoy reading about your life at camp. I can understand your feeling about all those deserted buildings—it reminds me of that scene in *The*

Best Years of Our Lives, where the airman gets a job as a junk remover on a disused airfield and found himself among those thousands of deserted airplanes.

I shall look forward to seeing your pictures. You said you visited a small "jerk-water" town. I have an idea that is a slang expression, but perhaps it means the town is a sort of spa, where people come to take the waters.

The drunken brawl you described sounds absolutely horrible—you picture it as just a normal sort of end to the fortnight's camp—as the usual thing. If anything like that happened in England, I should think there would be a frightful uproar

I went to an old-fashioned music hall the other night to see a show called *The Late Joys*. It's sponsored by the Players Theatre Club, and girls from the Club often get invitations. It's all supposed to take place in the last century, and before the performance there is a toast to Queen Victoria. I have been several times now and enjoy it immensely.

I am spending the weekend with my Aunt and Grandfather at Gillingham in Kent. It's about 40 miles from London, and quite a change, as they lead very quiet lives. They are quite religious, and I shall have to go to church twice today. My relatives are awfully strict about Sundays. I didn't have such a strict upbringing—I was forced to go to Sunday School until I was twelve, when my mother gave way to my constant rebellion.

Sincerely, Stephanie

◆   ◆   ◆

London, 16th September 1948
Dear Paul,

I was very glad to receive your last two letters, and I promise I won't write such things again as I did in mine of the 3rd. I realize now that my letter must have sounded very selfish, but I have buried the thought of it, and don't let's mention it again.

You seem to have saved quite a lot of money. If you save $40 a week, that's more than twice my week's earnings!

It was rather odd that you should mention in your letter about the possibilities of another war. We were only talking about it last night in our room. Somehow, it seems as though we wouldn't have a dog's chance if a war was declared, but it was like that in 1939, and we managed it somehow.

Reading your letter where you speak of being alone gave me another train of thought. I often wonder if I am really happy. I think the happiest days of my life were in 1941 when I lived on the Isle of Wight, but I am sure I am never actually happy now. I just seem to wish my life away—wishing for this and wishing for that—never really being satisfied.

I have ready to send you three of Agatha Christie's Penguins, which I hope you will enjoy reading. Also, I am including another current catalogue of Penguin Books.

Last evening I went to see a film called *Holiday Camp*. I loved every minute of it! I suppose I ought to tell you something about Holiday Camps. Since the war, all over Britain a new type of holiday resort has been springing up. A suitable piece of land beside the sea is purchased, and the Holiday Camp firm erects hundreds of chalets, ballrooms, swimming pools, golf courses, tennis courts, a theatre and numerous other entertainments. Some camps are small, and others, like the Butler chain, are huge, accommodating five to six thousand people! From morning to night there's always something on—a hike, a tour, a beauty competition, daily dozens, concerts, dances, etc. All day long loudspeakers are blaring at you to join in this and have a bash at that! You are awakened in the morning with "Good morning campers! Get up and have some fun!" In the evening they tell you, "Goodnight campers! Had a nice Day?" Everybody shouts "Ye—es!" It's not my type of vacation, but millions enjoy it.

Sincerely, Stephanie

◆   ◆   ◆

Akron, September 21, 1948
Dear Stephanie,

The Snow Goose arrived last week. Your wish was more than fulfilled, because I liked it very much. I can never thank you enough for sending it.

About the hotels: I think the Cumberland sounds best of all the ones you have mentioned. They do have private baths and breakfast is included in the rate of 17 shillings. Reservations can wait until January.

You are right in that "jerk-water town" is a slang expression, meaning a small, unimportant place. How it originated, I don't know really.

Yesterday I had one of the easiest days ever at work. I went with one of the bricklayers to the Colonial Theatre, where he installed a window of glass block. I had very little to do, and so in the afternoon I sat in the balcony and watched Betty Grable in *That Lady in Ermine*. It was a lousy film, but I can't complain—I was being paid $1.45 an hour while watching it!

Where are those pictures you were going to send? I enclose several more of me taken at camp.

I intend to have a concert on records tonight before I go to bed, so I guess I'll go downstairs and put on Beethoven's *Pastoral Symphony* for a start…

'Nite, Paul

◆   ◆   ◆

Epsom, 26th September 1948
Dear Paul,

I had a look at the Cumberland Hotel the other day and it seemed extremely nice. It faces Hyde Park and is in London's best area. I think you will like it.

I am spending the weekend with a girlfriend of mine. One of her hobbies is to ring the church bells. I went with her this morning, and it was really interesting to watch all the ringers pulling the changes. Yesterday, we went to Windsor Castle. We looked over the State Apartments, saw the Queen's Dolls' House and other relics. We climbed a tall tower to admire the view of Eton College and the River Thames in the distance. You must see Windsor when you come.

We are having chicken for lunch and I must be off now to partake…

Yours, Stephanie

◆   ◆   ◆

Akron, September 30, 1948
Dear Stephanie,

I went up to Cleveland last Saturday and bought a few books. I was looking for some Sherwood Anderson titles and found a shop that had nearly all of his published works. I hope to go to Cleveland again this weekend to see the pre-Broadway production of Tennessee Williams' new play, *Summer and Smoke*.

A few days ago, Dennis talked me into going to see two re-issues of British films: *Four Feathers* and *Drums*. Have you ever seen them? As I told Dennis, they're a couple of bloody good films, or should I say good *bloody* films! I thought they both had the same purpose—to glorify war and imperialism. In *Four Feathers*, a man is branded a coward because he puts his own beliefs before his duty to England. He believes the campaign is unjust and uncalled for, but in the end he yields and aids in the fighting. For doing this, *I* would call him a coward. It takes a brave man to stick to his beliefs when everyone else thinks otherwise.

Thank you for the picture. You look as beautiful as ever, and those chimney tops in the background just fascinate me!

The days are whizzing by—winter will be here before I know it! Then spring—wonderful spring! When I look at my bankbook and realize that I have saved nearly half my fund, I don't need any more assurance that I will be in England in April!

'Nite, Paul

◆   ◆   ◆

Akron, October 3, 1948
Dear Stephanie,

"October has come again, has come again, and this world, this life, this time are stranger than a dream." Thomas Wolfe said it all in that line—one of my favorites!

Well now, the first thing is to tell you about *Summer and Smoke.*

Briefly, this is the plot: Alma is the daughter of a minister and has been brought up as a very proper, religious young lady. John, the boy next door, is the son of a doctor, and he eventually goes off to medical school. Alma has been in love with John, but when he comes home from school, he has turned into a drinking, gambling type. They have a few unsuccessful dates, after which John pursues the town's leading prostitute. The climax comes when John holds a wild drinking party, and his father ends up being shot. John has a long talk with Alma, trying to convince her that there is no such thing as a soul—he asks her to show it to him on the medical chart.

After this, things begin to change. Alma becomes ill and will see no one. Meantime, John has become respectable and has fallen in love with a chaste and charming young lady of the town. He also has come to believe in the soul! There is a final scene between John and Alma, during which she confesses she no longer believes in her religion! In the end, Alma is picked up by a traveling salesman and they go off together.

I don't know just what conclusions you can draw from the play, but it certainly was good drama and the acting was first-rate.

During one of the weekends of this month, I will be taking a trip to Buffalo, New York. Mom is going to visit relatives there. I will be going with her but will not stay as long as she will. Buffalo is a nice city. It has several museums, a symphony orchestra, and a number of bookshops. Niagara Falls is also nearby.

Well, it's time to take my regular Sunday walk down to the Union Depot to pick up the New York newspapers.

Yours, Paul

◆   ◆   ◆

London, 8th October 1948
Dear Paul,

Today is such a beautiful day that I am full of the joys of autumn. Do you too have that wild frosty tang in the morning and that kind, warm old fog in the evening that whispers to you on the way home from work of toasted muffins and a blazing fire?

How nice for you to be going to Buffalo and Niagara Falls. What will the family do for cooking without your mother?

Thanks a lot for the report on *Summer and Smoke*. From your description, I should think our censors will have a jolly good time over it if it ever comes to London! All plays have to go to the Lord Chamberlain's office first to be approved, but the censor is far more liberal and lets a lot pass that couldn't be allowed on the screen.

From a remark in one of your letters about having a small fire in the furnace, I gather your house is centrally heated. Is that the case in most Akron houses?

Well, I must leave you at this point to start making a fancy apron for my mother. It should be quite pretty when it is finished—I hope!

Yours, Stephanie

◆   ◆   ◆

Akron, October 10, 1948
Dear Stephanie,

Sunday has come again, and after several days of onethingafteranother, I can pause and take a breath or two.

Last night I was in Cleveland for the opening concert of the Cleveland Orchestra. After a long summer of only a few good radio concerts and having to rely on records, last night's concert probably sounded twice as good as it actually was! Oh, but it was good! I liked the Haydn best—the *88th Symphony.*

While I was in Cleveland, I bought a signed copy of *Streetcar Named Desire.* It was a leftover copy from an autograph party held during Williams' recent visit for the opening of *Summer and Smoke.*

To turn from good entertainment to the very worst, the best review of the film *Carmen* appeared in *Newsweek* magazine: "It isn't *Carmen*, and it isn't Bizet, but it *is* Rita Hayworth—in Technicolor!"

By "centrally heated," I assume you mean one furnace that heats the whole house. I'm afraid I've never heard of a house here that wasn't heated in that manner. Our fireplaces are mostly just decoration.

Yours, Paul

◆   ◆   ◆

Akron, October 13, 1948
Dear Stephanie,

On Monday night, President Truman was in town and I was on hand with my camera. I went down to the train depot to see him come in, but couldn't get close enough to take any pictures there. The president, his wife and daughter came out on the rear platform of the train, where they were greeted by a welcoming committee. After that, Truman shook hands with what seemed like hundreds of people.

I went down to Main Street to await the scheduled parade. When the president's car approached, I took several shots, but the best one (print enclosed) was the last, when I ran out into the street, to within ten feet of the car. The president saw me and smiled at the large Dewey button I was wearing—thus making a perfect picture!

Truman's speech at the Armory was typical of the undignified political ballyhoo he has been giving out over the past month. I often wonder what people of other countries think when they hear our politicians speak!

I have just finished reading Aldous Huxley's *Brave New World*, and it has left me with a variety of feelings. The purpose of the book is to show how futile a Utopian world would be. And the most interesting thing is that since Huxley wrote the book (about 15 years ago) many of his predictions already have come into being. You really must read it!

In reference to the Buffalo trip, I'm afraid the family will have to eat out or fix for themselves while I'm away. As far as that goes, they can continue to do so when I come back! I like to cook, but not after working all day.

The other morning we had quite a fog outside. I was telling Freddy (the Englishman bricklayer) that I thought maybe we were in London. Well, I had to listen to a lecture on what real fogs are like! Freddy also came up with a good joke that is worth repeating: It seems that Pat was a Socialist and Mike was not. They were talking one day and Mike said to Pat, "Do you mean that if you had two houses you'd give me one?" "Sure," said Pat. "And if you had two horses, you'd give me one?" "Oh yes," said Pat. "If you had two pigs, would you give me one?" "Go on," said Pat. "You *know* I've got two pigs!"

Bye for now, Paul

◆   ◆   ◆

London, 20th October 1948
Dear Paul,

I was very amused by your description of photographing Mr. Truman! You certainly were awful wearing that large Dewey button—I really don't know how you had the nerve to run out to him wearing the other party's colours.

Thanks for the map of Indiana and the Middle West. One thing that amazed me is, although Indiana is the next state to Ohio, Indianapolis seems to be about 250–300 miles from Akron! I just can't fathom the size of America! When I look at the scale on the map, I realize how great the distances are—it really is amazing.

I'm getting ready for Christmas early this year. Sonia and I always make our mother a stocking full of different gifts, and we have more fun seeing her open them on Christmas Day than when we open our own things. I hope to hear *The Messiah* at the Albert Hall this year. I am fond of the music, and we did it one year at school.

Talking of school theatricals, did you do much of that sort of thing in high school? In secondary school, when I was 11, we did something about the life of Shakespeare, and I was thrilled to have a part. Another time we did *Macbeth* and I was first witch. Others we did were *Alice in Wonderland* (I played the Mad Hatter), and *Twelfth Night*, where (being tall) I was Sir Andrew Aguecheek! That turned out terribly funny!

There was quite a crowd in the street today, when an American car—a Studebaker—was the center of attention. I am not keen on it myself, as you can't see whether it is coming or going!

I usually receive letters from you on Thursday afternoons these days, so perhaps I'll get one tomorrow. Though I don't think I really deserve one, do I? I have slacked off lately, I know. Anyway, cheerio for a short while.

Sincerely, Stephanie

♦   ♦   ♦

Akron, October 28, 1948
Dear Stephanie,

I arrived home from Buffalo this morning. I had a great time there, visiting the museums and browsing in the bookstores. I found a copy of *All Quiet on the Western Front*, which I have been wanting for some time. One evening I went to see a new movie, *Johnny Belinda*. Put that on your must see list! I'll bet you do some crying before it's over!

Mother went with me to Niagara Falls on Monday, but the weather was miserably cold. The next day I visited the Science Museum, where they have an interesting glass man. I purchased a few booklets at the museum, including one entitled, *How to Fall in Love Intelligently*. Does that sound possible to you? Of course it's all about heredity, etc.

A letter from you was waiting when I got home, so I'd better see what comments I should make.

I'm afraid we don't produce Shakespeare in our American high schools. Mostly we do variety shows, with the choir, solos, skits, dancing acts, boy and girl songs, etc.

You say you don't deserve a letter from me. You deserve ten times the amount I do write! I will be writing more in the future though, since we have to start planning my trip before long.

Yours, Paul

◆   ◆   ◆

London, 4th November 1948
Dear Paul,

Well, well, well! I'm just longing to hear what you have to say about the American election results. I have never been so amazed in all my life! Today's papers are full of it. *The Express* has published a very touching article about Truman under the headline, "He ain't no Churchill, but what the heck!"

Thank you for your letter with commentary on your Buffalo trip. Judging by the picture you sent it seems to be a lovely town.

Yes, I should like to see *Johnny Belinda*—odd title! I am very fond of Jane Wyman as well as Lew Ayres.

I went to a lunch hour concert at St. George's Church, Bloomsbury, on Tuesday last. I didn't get a programme, owing to the reason that I was trying to economize, so I can't tell you what they played except that they were works by Mozart, Tchaikovsky and Grieg. The performance was given by the string section of the New London Symphony Orchestra, and I enjoyed it very much.

Cheerio for now, Stephanie

Right: Cecil
Residential Club,
195-201 Gower
Street, London.

*"Cecil House was
built in 1939 by Mrs.
Chesterton and
subscribers. It
wasn't used for its
original purpose until
1946, for the war
intervened and the
building was used
for the Canadian
Army. It now houses
72 girls."*

Below: Stephanie
(right) posing with
friend Beryl on the
roof of the Cecil
Club.

Above: "Greenacre," in Merstham, Surrey, where Stephanie's mother was employed as a live-in housekeeper.

Right: Stephanie poses in the garden at Greenacre, 1948.

"I am home in Merstham for the holiday weekend. It is a beautiful day, the sky is blue, the sun is brilliant, the flowers are beautiful and I feel in love with the whole world."

Left: Paul Duke in 1948.

I'm enclosing a picture of yours truly. I do quite a bit of photography— developing my own film and making my own prints."

Below: The attic room at 696 Hazel Street. Where Paul wrote to Stephanie on the old Underwood typewriter in the foreground.

Above: 696 Hazel Street, Akron, Ohio, photographed in 1948.

Below: President Harry Truman campaigning in Akron, October 1948. *"When the president's car approached, I took several shots, but the best one was the last when I ran out into the street to within ten feet of the car."*

Akron, November 4, 1948
Dear Stephanie,

I was as surprised as any other American when I heard the news of Truman's victory. I guess his fighting campaign was responsible. The Democrats will also have a majority in Congress, and if they live up to their platform, they will do more for the working people than the Republicans would have done.

I have been thinking about the trip. Not long ago you were saying, "But it seems such a long way off!" The way time has been going, April will be here before I know it. So let's start making some plans, shall we? I see the airlines have reduced the NY-London fare to $466 for the off-season. In January I will get a passport, make plane reservations and you can make the hotel reservation at that time too. Also, I want to start sending you some money so you can do some advance buying of tickets for concerts, plays, etc.

I hope to hear from you tomorrow, but you are probably getting even with me for not writing while in Buffalo.

Bye for now, Paul

◆   ◆   ◆

London, 8th November 1948
Dear Paul,

Coming home from work this evening, I noticed the lighting along Gower Street. Everywhere around our side of the Tottenham Court Road is gaslit, and a lamplighter still goes round every night and morning to turn the lights on and off. Do you have any gas lights in Akron?

I do agree with you that we should think ahead about the trip. As to booking theatre seats, would you like an estimate of prices? The gallery costs two shillings and sixpence (fifty cents), upper circle, five or six shillings ($1.00), dress circle ten shillings and sixpence to thirteen shillings and sixpence ($2 and $3), and stalls are from six shillings to sixteen shillings ($1.00 to $3.25). How do they tally with your prices?

I had better tell you that however much I would like to have more than two weeks holiday during your visit, that will be the maximum time allowed to me. I don't usually work on Saturdays though.

Thank you for the pictures you sent. The mounted pictures were wizard and I especially enjoyed the scenes of the Pennsylvania countryside. I sent you a couple of maps the other day—one of London and the other of England and Wales.

Goodbye for awhile, Stephanie

◆   ◆   ◆

Akron, November 14, 1948
Dear Stephanie,

Brrrrrrrr! I don't think winter has officially arrived, but we had our first snow this week, and the days are getting colder all the time. Winter is sneaking up on you too, according to your letter. I enjoyed reading about the lamplighters. We don't have any gaslights in Akron.

Thanksgiving Day will soon be here and we are invited out to my brother Bruce's house for a turkey dinner. I remember when we had two Thanksgiving Days. When Roosevelt was president, he had the date set back a week, but a lot of people didn't want to give up the old date. So we had "Roosevelt's Turkey Day" as well as the regular Thanksgiving!

About my visit: I'm wondering about trips I might take that will last more than a day. Say I decided to stay at Stratford for a day or so, would you be able to come along and do likewise? Or is that sort of thing frowned upon?

Fred Allen came up with a pretty good show last Sunday, with some amusing comments on the election. During his regular stroll down "Allen's Alley," Senator Claghorn said to him, "Son, this country hasn't seen such a turn-over since the *Normandie* went over on its side! And the public opinion polls! Why this is the first time in history that the poles went to the dogs!"

Bye for now, Paul

◆   ◆   ◆

London, 17th November 1948
Dear Paul,

Thank you for your latest letter. I haven't thanked you either for the *Life* magazines you have been sending. You have no idea of the enjoyment we get out of the magazines you send—we all read them in our room and then pass them on for others to read.

For the past week we have been completely smothered by thick fog—the sort of fog Americans seem to imagine always covers London. It is so penetrating too. At the Club it seeps in through the doors and windows and floats down the corridors and into the rooms!

In answer to your question about trips that last longer than a day, people are pretty tolerant about that sort of thing nowadays, I think. I had to ask my mother of course, what she thought, and she was quite in agreement.

At the moment I am waiting with eagerness for the film *Red River* to appear on the scene. There are many posters about, picturing vivid, flaming arrows and galloping horses. Anne says I have the cinema taste of a boy of ten! But I don't really think so—it's only that I get much more enjoyment out of a good western than I ever get out of those wretched, half-baked romances and musicals which take up so much of the cinema screen.

Sincerely, Stephanie

◆   ◆   ◆

Akron, November 24, 1948
Dear Stephanie,

Your map of England is spread out on my bed, and I have been studying it carefully. If you were impressed by the immensity of my country, I am equally impressed by the smallness of yours! It is an excellent map, and I am able to locate places and calculate distances quite easily. The other day I got so worked up about my trip as I studied the folders and maps that I could hardly sleep that night.

I heard from British Overseas Airlines the other day. They sent along a number of folders, including one that states that laundry can and does take as long as three weeks in Britain! If that is so, I shall have to bring along a lot of clothes to last me out!

At the present time, I am doing something I shouldn't be doing—worrying. Worrying mostly about unforeseen expenses on my trip, and will I have enough money? Oh well, I guess everything will work out somehow—it has to!

Some of those guided tours of Shakespeare Country look good. I think several days in the Midlands would be worthwhile.

Bye for now, Paul

◆   ◆   ◆

London, 30th November 1948
Dear Paul,

I received your latest letter, with plans for your trip.

Today I phoned the Cumberland to find the answer to a question that seems to be bothering you. They said laundry takes 4 days, and express service will do it in two days. I do think it rather silly of BOAC to say that laundry takes three weeks or more—it is neither encouraging nor does it give a good impression.

This is a good time to ask how much money you intend to bring with you. I will have some money saved by then, as well, as I couldn't possibly sponge on you to pay for everything. It's un-British!

I have come to the conclusion that I should have my two weeks off at least a week after you come, in order that we can get to know each other first. Because let's face it, it's going to be very different meeting in person than just corresponding, don't you think?

I must close for now, to go down to the kitchen and join the hot water bottle queue!

Bye for now, Stephanie

◆   ◆   ◆

Akron, December 5, 1948
Dear Stephanie,

On Saturday I went up to Cleveland to see Maurice Evans' production of Shaw's *Man and Superman*. I thought it was one of the wittiest plays I have ever seen, and Maurice Evans was superb!

Time is flying by, and it can keep right on flying as long as it slows down a bit in April!

I am relieved to hear about the laundry situation. You ask about how much money I will be bringing with me. It will be at least $400, and at the most $600. I have outlined my bank deposits and expenses for the remaining weeks, and it all looks good at the moment.

And don't worry about me paying for things. After all, I started this whole thing, and I certainly don't want to be a drain on your hard-earned savings. If it's un-British for you to accept, I'm afraid it's un-American for me not to insist otherwise!

'Night, Paul

◆   ◆   ◆

London, 10th December 1948
Dear Paul,

If you are bringing $400 with you, it does seem to be enough. In regard to my own money situation, I shall save as hard as I can until April comes—and I think it will work out all right.

Thank you for the picture you sent. Although I really can't judge, it seems to be a good one. I love the tie—is that one of those that will knock my eyes out?

To get around to more everyday things, I should like to hear more about your work. I have only the haziest ideas about what you do. I should think your work is certainly a good toughening up system for your future stay in Austerity-Britain!

Sincerely, Stephanie

◆   ◆   ◆

Akron, December 15, 1948
Dear Stephanie,

You ask about my work. Laboring is a job that any moron with a strong back and weak mind can do. Mostly, I build scaffolds for the bricklayers and supply them with brick and mortar. I used to hate it, but now I don't mind at all. Payday follows payday, and I am swimming in money! I don't know how long I will continue in construction work—maybe I will go to photography school or something like that. Anyway, for now it suits me. Youth isn't a time to be slaving over college textbooks and always planning for a distant future. When I get old they can take me out and shoot me if I am useless. I want my good times now, when I can really appreciate them!

I have most of my Christmas shopping done—thank goodness! No, we don't have Christmas puddings over here—we usually have pumpkin and mince pies for the holidays.

Have sent you off an *America in Color* calendar for the New Year.

Goodnight, Paul

◆   ◆   ◆

London, 18th December 1948
Dear Paul,

I must thank you for the books I received a couple of days ago. I love *The Thurber Carnival*. Last night, Joan read aloud some extracts from it, and we were howling with laughter—practically collapsing!

You should be receiving a *Merrie England* calendar shortly. You might not hear from me again this side of Christmas. I'll wish you now all good wishes for Christmas—and don't eat too much!

Sincerely, Stephanie

◆   ◆   ◆

Akron, December 19, 1948
Dear Stephanie,

I went to the travel agency yesterday and worked out a schedule based on the excursion airfare. I will be leaving New York on March 31, and return home on April 27. My reservations at the Cumberland would start April 1 and end on April 27, with about a week reserved in the middle of the month for a tour up north. If this seems OK to you, go ahead and make the reservations.

Tonight I'll have to go out and buy a Christmas tree. We usually put it up a few days before Christmas and leave the packages there until Christmas morning. I'll be taking pictures of our holiday and will send them to you if they are any good.

Sincerely, Paul

◆   ◆   ◆

The Office, 23rd December 1948
Dear Paul,

The weather is bitterly cold here, but we haven't had any snow yet. This office is none too warm either, as there is only a gas fire, and the generous Government has a habit of cutting down gas and electricity to a low level—especially when the weather is at its coldest. So it is a very cold person who is writing this letter.

That was quite a speech you made in your letter, and your comment at the end of it was exceedingly funny, I thought. I can quite agree with most of your sentiments, but you seem to concentrate on youth and old age, and you don't mention a word of what you will do with yourself over the twenty odd years in between!

Speaking of old age, every day when I come to the office I pass a poor old woman selling matches in the street—even in this cold weather. All over London there are old men drawing pictures on the pavements or just hanging around with notices on their necks, "blind," "deaf and dumb," etc. Many of them seem to make a living out of barrel organ playing or playing the spoons. Do you have "down and outs" like that in the States?

I heard Handel's *Messiah* on Tuesday last at the Albert Hall. It was a rare and wonderful performance. Last night, a performance by the Huddersfield Choral Society, conducted by Malcom Sargent was relayed over the radio, so I listened to the whole of it again.

Sincerely, Stephanie

◆   ◆   ◆

Akron, December 27, 1948
Dear Stephanie,

With the family spread out so much this year, we had a rather dull Christmas—not so much fuss over rituals and decorations. My presents were all clothes as I requested—I'll need them for my trip.

I had a bumper mail from you today—a letter, the calendar, and a Christmas card. Thank you for the photos enclosed with your letter. Your Club certainly is a modernistic looking building! Your sister Sonia looks like a girl who lives a few doors away from us, who also runs around all the time in slacks. I think they look horrible!

Bye for now, Paul

◆   ◆   ◆

London, New Year's Day, 1949
Dear Paul,

Happy New Year! It's the wettest, horriblest day imaginable here in London. The rain keeps pouring down as if it will never stop. I have decided to stay in London for the weekend.

I had quite a pleasant Christmas with plenty of good things to eat. It wouldn't be Christmas without the jolly old plum pudding, and my mother's turned out very well. Just before it is served in all its black and fruity splendor, brandy is poured over it and then set alight. A blue flame springs up all round it for several minutes. Inside the pudding are many different things—silver charms and six-penny pieces.

I am in the middle of making your reservations at the Cumberland and will send you their statement at the earliest moment. After much thought I must say that I will not accompany you on your tour north. Now that is final, so don't write anything in objection to it. I am willing to take a holiday for two of the weeks you are in the south, when London districts can be visited and day trips into the country can be made.

Cheerio for the present, Stephanie

◆   ◆   ◆

Akron, January 4, 1949
Dear Stephanie,

I have made my reservation with American Overseas Airlines and expect to have confirmation tomorrow. This morning I went downtown and bought two suitcases for my trip—they are made of aluminum. So things are moving along!

The past few days have been like spring around here, with continual rain. We have used up our inside work, so I hope I don't lose too much time (and money) on the job because of the rain. From this point forward, I shall be very tight with my money!

Most of my Christmas pictures didn't turn out well, but I will have some to send you.

'Til next time, Paul

◆   ◆   ◆

London, 4th January 1949
Dear Paul,

I enclose statements received from the Cumberland Hotel yesterday evening. I have made enquiries about the food rationing notes fixed to the letters, and I find overseas visitors are able to stay a month here without presenting any ration books at all. However, if you want your sweet ration when you are here, you must present your passport to the Food Office and they will allow you up to a pound of sweets for the month. I have asked for your room to overlook Hyde Park, as I think you would like that.

Yesterday was the first day of our six-page newspapers. The Government are now permitting six pages to be published three days a week, instead of the usual four pages we have had since the war. It certainly is a step forward, and we are all quite thrilled. I have sent you a packet of the main papers produced yesterday.

Sincerely, Stephanie

P.S. Take care of the reservations!

◆   ◆   ◆

Akron, January 10, 1949
Dear Stephanie,

Your letter with the reservations arrived today, and you can bet your boots I will guard them carefully! Thanks for requesting the room overlooking Hyde Park—that's something I never would have thought about.

The Liberty Theatre is going back to showing foreign films full time. I saw *The Mozart Story* the other night, but it was lousy. Speaking of Mozart, reminds me that I ran across another Stephanie the other day. *He* wrote the libretto for Mozart's *Abduction From the Seraglio*. And since he is Stephanie the Younger, I assume there must have been a Stephanie the elder as well!

If you have made up your mind not to go on the tour of the countryside, no amount of argument on my part will persuade you otherwise. Only, of course, I'm disappointed.

Thank you so much for all the trouble you went to in getting the reservations for me. It's a wonderful feeling to know that all these dates are now definite and no longer cloudy dreams. In one of your letters you said you would tell me more about something when you see me. How often I have felt the same way—how much easier it will be when we can talk instead of write! And it won't be long now, will it? Just think! Only 80 days, 15 hours and ten minutes from now I'll be "setting my watch by Big Ben," as one of my travel folders says! Oh joy!

Sincerely, Paul

◆   ◆   ◆

London, January 15th 1949
Dear Paul,

Your calendar finally arrived. It is beautiful! Thank you very much indeed. I am sending you a copy of *The Good Companions* by Priestly. It's only a second-hand copy I'm afraid—I bought it from Foyles the other day.

You have heard of the death of Tommy Handley, I expect. There is not another man in the country—Churchill or anyone—who has had such love and affection from so many people. When I heard *Memories From ITMA* on the radio last night, I had a great lump in my throat.

I saw *Red River* the other day and naturally enjoyed it muchly. Anne went to see it too—her first large-scale western—and I am glad to say that even she liked it. John Wayne was superb!

Though I would like to meet you at the airport, I don't know whether I shall be able. In any case, I shall have the first Saturday and Sunday off. What would you like to do on those days? There will be all sorts of things to see and do. I am sending you some pamphlets about what is likely to be on in the theatres—the Old Vic, with Olivier and Leigh, will be starting soon, and there will be opera and ballet at Covent Garden. Anyway, you can pick out the things you would like to see.

I am really very sorry you are so disappointed that I am not coming on your tour. I thought somehow you would be able to read between the lines. The more I thought about it, the more it seemed to be unwise. Anyway, after about a fortnight in London, you will be jolly glad to get away from me, I'm quite sure.

T.T.F.N., Stephanie

◆   ◆   ◆

Akron, January 23, 1949
Dear Stephanie,

Well, cross another item off the list! The passport has been duly applied for and I should have it in a few weeks' time.

I have been thinking quite a lot about the trip lately. Your suggestions as to what to do during my time in London are all very good. I think it might be a good idea to take an organized tour around London on the Saturday—my first full day.

There are quite a few things I have been meaning to ask you and then I forget! One thing comes to mind: Freddie says that Leicester is pronounced "Lester." Is that right? And how about the river Thames? I have always pronounced it the way it looks, but I suppose that is wrong too! I'm relying on you to set me straight when I goof!

I hadn't heard of the death of Tommy Handley. I suppose it would be the same here if Jack Benny or Bob Hope died.

Sincerely, Paul

◆   ◆   ◆

London, January 28ᵗʰ 1949
Dear Paul,

My goodness! I have never been so amazed as when I read your pronunciation of Thames! You must never pronounce it as it is spelt! It is *Temms*. As for other places, Leicester is Lester, Gloucester is Gloster, Worcester is Wooster, and Worcestershire is Woostersheer.

I have heard a lot about American hamburgers, but I don't know exactly what they are like. Are they a roll with ham in the middle?

We had an "American Day" at school when I was eleven. Americans came to speak to us, we sang American songs, and acted an American version of *The Three Bears.* Just as the play was beginning, an air-raid siren went and we were all hustled off to the shelter, and nobody bothered about the play after that!

I have sent off the T.S. Eliot book of poems that you wanted.

Sincerely, Stephanie

◆   ◆   ◆

Akron, February 14, 1949
Dear Stephanie,

Enclosed you will find (I hope!) the sum of two pounds. I will be sending more in the weeks ahead so that you will have money in hand to buy theatre tickets. I find I can buy pounds here in Akron for $3.25 each, so I should send as many as possible before I leave.

I have a book of poems by A.E. Housman out of the library, and I am really enjoying his verse. I'm also reading Eliot's *Murder in The Cathedral,* in preparation for my visit to Canterbury. Thank you for sending the copy of *The Good Companions*—I shall be reading that next.

Only 45 days until I leave! I have my passport now, my vaccination certificate, and my plane ticket and hotel reservations. And oh yes, did I tell you that Freddy has a son and family who live in Birmingham? I have been invited to stay with them during my week up north.

Sincerely, Paul

◆   ◆   ◆

Merstham, 19th February 1949
Dear Paul,

You wouldn't guess where I am while writing this letter—out in the garden, with the sun shining down!

First of all, the money reached me safely—you could have bowled me over with a feather when I opened your letter and the pounds fell out! I shall keep a book of the money you send and make full debit and credit accounts of it all. I enclose herewith a list of all the London theatres, with shows ticked that are likely to be on when you are here. I'm sure you would probably like to see *The Heiress*, because it is by Henry James, and it stars Ralph Richardson.

I have a confession to make. Without consulting you I went ahead and booked for *Swan Lake*, with Margot Fonteyn and Robert Helpmann. However, I shan't do that again unless I have your confirmation.

Last Sunday I stayed in London and went with some friends to an all-Beethoven concert at the Albert Hall. The program included the *Eroica Symphony* and the *Emperor Piano Concerto*—it was all very stirring! Do you find it hard to say how you enjoy the concerts that you hear? I'm afraid I do—I haven't enough adjectives at my command to do the music justice. When I write, "it was wonderful, enthralling, etc.," it looks so commonplace and mean written down on paper.

I have been thinking the contents of this next paragraph over a lot and have finally decided to include it, although I shall hate myself when I have posted this letter. Oh well, here goes: Do you think when you come you could possibly include in your luggage some nylon stockings and a packet of Oxydol for me? There, I've said it now—what you think of me I have no idea! Naturally, I'll pay you for them when you get here, but it's just the thought of asking you to bring them.

Sincerely, Stephanie

Akron, March 3, 1949
Dear Stephanie,

Glad to hear the pound notes have been arriving safely. Please don't worry about having booked *Swan Lake*—I am very glad you did! Go ahead and book *The Heiress, Edward, My Son*, and all three plays at the Old Vic. What about opera at Covent Garden? Anything doing in April?

As for your request, I'll be glad to bring some nylons and the Oxydol soap with me. You'll have to tell me the size of the nylons, so please do so as soon as possible.

I have more to write about, but perhaps I'll write again in a day or two. Can I enter a complaint that I don't hear from you quite so often these days?

Sincerely, Paul

◆   ◆   ◆

London, 4ᵗʰ March 1949
Dear Paul,

So far I have booked for *Richard III, The Heiress, Swan Lake,* and *Antigone*. I have found it very difficult to book for the Old Vic—I had to pay 15/6 ($3.00) each for those tickets! I hope you don't pass out at the cost! In getting seats for the other plays I will be able to pay less, I am sure. By the way, it seems as though you are going to a play or concert every night—is that what you want?

I'm enclosing a booklet from the Albert Hall with the April listings. Tell me please, what you want booked. I want to hear what concerts you would like to attend before I arrange any more theatres.

Sincerely, Stephanie

◆   ◆   ◆

Akron, 8ᵗʰ March 1949
Dear Stephanie,

Enclosed is a list of concerts to book. As to my first day in London, even if we do spend the day sightseeing, I would like to attend the Albert Hall concert. I don't tire easily, and I have no intention of wasting one single moment of my time in England!

I have just finished reading *Antigone*, and am looking forward to seeing the Old Vic production. According to *Time* magazine, Olivier does the chorus dressed in a dinner jacket!

Sincerely, Paul

◆   ◆   ◆

Merstham, 12th March 1949
Dear Paul,

It is very kind of you to say you will bring the stockings and I do thank you very much. The Oxydol, I thought afterwards, might be cumbersome, and it can be obtained on points over here. But soap is a thing I am always short of because although we are allowed 4 ounces a month, the Club automatically claims half our ration. So if you could possibly squeeze into your bag a couple of bars of toilet soap instead of the Oxydol, I should be most grateful. Oh yes, before I forget—the size of the nylons is ten English size—perhaps American sizes differ?

Well, it's a very short time, and I will be seeing you. Three weeks today, I shall actually be talking to you instead of writing! Isn't it amazing how these months have flown by?

Sincerely, Stephanie

◆   ◆   ◆

Akron, March 17, 1949
Dear Stephanie,

You have done very well with the bookings. If there is going to be an entertainment every night while I am in London, I can only say "Good!"

I have just been reading a travel book by Aldous Huxley—*Jesting Pilate*. In it he says something with which I completely agree:

"Everybody in the ship menaces us with the prospect of having 'a good time' in India. A good time means going to the races, playing bridge, drinking cocktails, dancing 'til four in the morning, and talking about nothing. And meanwhile, the beautiful, the incredible world in which we live awaits our exploration, and life is short…and there is all knowledge, all art. There are men and women, the innumerable living, and in books, the souls of those dead who deserve to be immortal. Heaven preserve me in such a world from having a good time!"

Did I tell you I wrote to Mrs. Bernstein (the real-life Esther in Thomas Wolfe's novels)? I wanted to know where in London Wolfe began to write *Look Homeward, Angel.* I had a very nice reply, in which she rambles on about Wolfe quite a bit.

Just over two weeks until I leave! I enclose a calendar for April, upon which you can record all the bookings, etc.

So long for awhile, Paul

◆   ◆   ◆

London, 19th March 1949
Dear Paul,

Have you read in your papers at all that London is to have the lights turned on again starting April 2nd? Isn't that just wonderful? It seems as if the Fuel Minister knew you were coming and decided to switch them on for you! I can't remember the lights being on before the war (the theatres, signs, cinemas, etc.) so it will be more of a novelty for me than for you.

I have put the Club telephone number at the top of this letter. I think the best thing for you to do is to ring me up at the Club at 6:00 on Friday evening, after your arrival.

Until I hear from you again, Stephanie

◆   ◆   ◆

Akron, March 20, 1949
Dear Stephanie,

Ten more days! Ten more days and I shall be off!

I got some nylons for you. They are very sheer, size ten, and a very neutral color, which should go with anything. The clerk was very helpful and said that the difference in size between English and American was not enough to make any difference.

I have ordered a dozen rolls of color film (96 pictures), and four dozen rolls of black-and-white (384 pictures). I hope that will be enough

Yesterday, my brother Ted was looking at one of my more colorful shirts, and his comment was: "You'll probably be arrested if you wear anything like that in England!" The shirt he was referring to is yellow, with little sea horses printed all over it. Ted is very conservative in his dress!

Bye for now, Paul

◆   ◆   ◆

London, 24th March 1949
Dear Paul,

As you requested, I am writing my last letter today.

First of all, I must apologize for not having confirmed that you have sent me twenty pounds altogether. Anyway, after all the bookings, I still have money in the region of 7 to 8 pounds to give you back.

The nylons you have bought do sound thrilling! With regard to your shirt with the seahorses all over them, although you wouldn't come to the point of being arrested, it certainly would provide people with anecdotes for a week or more. People in the street would go home and say: "You would never guess what I saw—a boy wearing a yellow shirt with some fantastic animals printed all over it—seahorses, I think! Can you imagine anything more frightful? Of course he was an American, you could see it at a glance." I know that's what I would say if I saw somebody wearing what you described!

Reading back over this letter, it doesn't seem to be up to the standard of what a "last letter" should be. But anyway, I hope you do have a safe journey over, and if all goes well I shall see you next Friday. So, until then,

Goodbye for now, Stephanie

◆   ◆   ◆

Akron, March 26, 1949
Dear Stephanie.

Well this is it! The last letter before I leave!

I simply cannot hold back the excitement any longer! I'm so excited I can't do anything very well, including the writing of this letter. Four days to go! For a long time I was used to the idea, and what with waiting and waiting and waiting, I couldn't work up much real excitement at all. But such is not the case now. I don't know how I'll live through these next four days!

I'm sure there are any number of things I should include in this letter, but I'm so worked up I can't think straight! Ah well...

Well, I guess it's goodbye for now, and the next time you hear from me it will be with a telephone receiver to your ear. Sit tight and keep your fingers crossed that I'll have a safe voyage!

Until next Friday then, I remain, sincerely yours, Paul

Part Two:
What Is Love?

Somewhere inside of me there is still a nineteen-year-old young man who surfaces every now and then to remind me of all the excitement, joy and sense of wonder I experienced during that trip to England in April of 1949.

I see myself once again on the 30ᵗʰ March, pacing the floor of the living room at 696 Hazel Street, impatiently awaiting the hour of departure for the Greyhound Bus Terminal in downtown Akron. Placing a stack of records on the phonograph, I amuse myself by "conducting" Brahms' Third Symphony—the soaring, climactic chords sending shivers of excitement down my spine. Later, on the night coach to New York City, moving ever eastward along the Pennsylvania Turnpike, the music continues to spin endlessly around in my head: da-da-da-dee-dum, da-da-da-dee-dum! Sleep is impossible.

On the following afternoon I board an American Overseas Airlines Constellation aircraft at La Guardia Field. It is supposed to be a non-stop flight, but headwinds necessitate stops to refuel at Gander, Newfoundland, Reykjavik, Iceland, and Shannon, Ireland. The prop-driven plane takes nearly twenty-four hours to reach London.

Exhausted from all the excitement and lack of sleep, I feel very much a stranger in a strange land as I check into the posh-looking Cumberland Hotel. All attempts to reach Stephanie by phone yield only a busy signal. (Only one phone for all those girls?) After a quick refreshing bath, I resolve to walk to the Cecil Club—I simply must make contact with Stephanie that night!

It is late in the evening when Stephanie and I finally meet face-to-face in the lobby of the Cecil Club. We smile, shake hands, and chat away like old friends—bringing each other up to date and reviewing our plans for the days ahead. I return to my hotel that night in high spirits—thrilled to be in England at last and convinced that Stephanie and I would get on well together.

And get on well we did. With the exception of the week I spent in the Midlands, Stephanie was my constant guide and companion. Over the long Easter weekend, and during a week that Stephanie arranged to have off from work, we made day trips to such places as Dover, Brighton, Stratford, and the Isle of Wight.

Every evening we attended some kind of theatrical entertainment. Seated amid the glittering splendor of the Royal Opera House, we watched Margot Fonteyn dance in Swan Lake; *at the Albert Hall we attended a Beethoven/Tchaikovsky concert conducted by the legendary Sir Thomas Beecham; and within the intimate confines of the New Theatre, we sat spellbound in the presence of Richard III, as portrayed by Sir Laurence Olivier.*

On days when Stephanie had to work, I explored London on my own. I prowled among the antiquities in the British Museum, strolled along Fleet Street and The

Strand in the footsteps of Boswell and Johnson, and spent hours browsing in the book-shops in Bloomsbury and Charing Cross Road.

At the Cumberland Hotel, I placed my shoes outside my door each night (to be polished by some unseen pair of hands), and had breakfast every morning at "the Gentlemen's Table," where waiters in formal attire served each course from juice to toast and marmalade with great ceremony.

As one day followed another, I lived each moment to the full—scarcely able to think of the past or future. Racing along Oxford Street to and from the Cumberland, or strolling hand-in-hand with Stephanie through the lush, green countryside of the poets, there was only the here and now to be considered.

It was not until the final hours that I was forced to face up to my imminent departure. With a heavy heart, I boarded the plane for New York on the 27th of April. It seemed to me that I was leaving behind everything I most loved in life—and in particular, a girl named Stephanie...

...In flight with American Airlines
10:00 PM, 27th April 1949
Dear Stephanie,

I hardly know where to begin. I am on a monstrous machine that is taking me thousands of miles away from you.

Did you stay to see us take off? After I left you I had to wait in the passengers' lounge for nearly an hour, and I never spent a more miserable hour in my life! Parting may be "sweet sorrow," but I don't mean to be parted from you again. The next time I hold you in my arms you won't get away—ever!

It's getting dark, the people have quieted down, and we are traveling along quite smoothly at 274 miles per hour. We are on our way to Iceland. I have an idea that just about every flight ends up stopping there. I have met no one of interest on the plane. Ah well, I don't feel very sociable anyway.

I won't sleep tonight. I wonder about you. Oh God, but I miss you!

We are now at Iceland. I'm mailing this off to you as is.

All my love, Paul

◆   ◆   ◆

Merstham, 29th April 1949
Dear Paul,

I wonder where you are now. I suppose still traveling ever farther away from me.

You know, I just didn't get used to the idea that you were going—even right at the end when you kissed me goodbye, I just felt numb. When I went back to the field alone to wait, the truth came over me, and I felt so miserable.

It seemed to take an age for the plane to come back along the runway. When it came whizzing by our enclosure, it was so fast—a second passed and it was gone. I watched the plane right out into the distance, until it just merged into nothingness. I felt very lonely then, and it frightened me that you could be whisked out of England at such a speed.

I caught the Greenline coach straight back to London. I was still dry-eyed then, and when I had my supper, but when I got upstairs again and back to my room, something snapped and I just had to cry. Did you think it hard of me not to have cried at the airport? I hope not, because anyway, it would have been much harder for you.

Have you come to your senses by now? About me, I mean! Please think it over very carefully and try not to love me (as I believe you said the other evening). But if you feel you love me a little, don't let it become exaggerated, which is likely to happen when you are so far away. Instead, try to think of all the faults about me that you can, so that if or when we meet again you won't be too disappointed.

I am feeling all mixed up and lonely now, wondering what the future will hold. Oh, Paul, I miss you very much. Did we gain anything or lose anything during the past month? It is terrifying to think of all these empty months to come. Oh, how I wish I knew how to be in love and what it is!

I shan't write again until I hear from you, and I hope that is soon.

So dear Paul, until then,
Much love from Stephanie

◆   ◆   ◆

Akron, May 1, 1949
Dear Stephanie,

I'm home again and I hate it—all of it! Oh to be back in England!

I suppose I'd better review the trip home first. For the most part I was alone with my thoughts—all I could think about for hours and hours was you riding back alone into London. At Iceland they have opened up a new terminal building, which is quite luxurious—I think I sent you a postcard as well as a letter from there. When I got back on the plane I felt so exhausted and miserable, I fell asleep in spite of everything. After waking and dozing a number of times, I discovered we were preparing to land at Labrador of all places! From there to New York was a matter of about four hours. The bus trip back to Akron was hard to take. I'm certain I will fly all the way next time.

What else can I write about? Words are so futile! If only I could put my arms around you and kiss you! In general I hate everyone and everything around me here—and I hate this house because it will be my prison until I see you again.

I'll feel much better at work tomorrow, because as the days go by and the money rolls in, I know that every day and every dollar will be bringing me closer to you. As for the future, what do you think we ought to do? When should I come again, and are you sure you won't let me bring you here? We have ages to think about all that, but it will be nice when we have a plan.

I wonder if you have found it as hard to write as I am finding it. I don't know how I will live until next Tuesday, when I should hear from you. I should get busy in my darkroom tonight, and perhaps I will. I really can't put my heart into anything because I no longer have it. YOU have it—and you and my heart are thousands of miles away!

Forever yours, Paul

♦   ♦   ♦

Akron, May 4, 1949
Dear Stephanie,

I thought I would go crazy waiting to hear from you, and now that I have your letter of last Friday, I feel ever so much better.

You ask if I have come to my senses—about you, that is. Stephanie, if you don't want me to use the word "love," I suppose I needn't, but what else can I say? Why don't you want me to love you? Why do you want me to think of your faults? I don't understand—really, I don't. You're the best and truest friend I've ever had—I love you—I need you—I want you! If only I could make you understand!

Oh, Stephanie, this letter's a mess! I can't write what I want to say. Darling, you've got to write me lots and lots and try to straighten me out. Forgive me for not writing the pages and pages you deserve. Oh, I ache all over and I can't talk to this damned piece of paper! I want you—you—you!

Your lonely Paul

♦   ♦   ♦

London, 5th May 1949
Dear Paul,

First I received your postcard from New York, then yesterday I had your letter from Iceland, and today your letter from Akron came. You had quite a trip evidently! Fancy going right up to Labrador!

Like you, I hated everybody, and at work I simply loathed them all. Over the weekend I was so miserable—goodness knows what I wrote in that letter I sent you on Saturday. Anyway, I do miss you, Paul, more than I ever thought I would. I think of you all the time and there are moments when I just long for you to be here with me.

When shall we meet again? In thunder, lightening or in rain? I have been thinking quite a lot, and I have come to the conclusion that I could probably save up enough to go to America in 1 1/2—2 years. I couldn't go by air, but a ship passage would cost only about 50 pounds. With another 50 pounds to spend, how long would that last in America? Two weeks?

Oh, aren't letters stupid and inadequate! Like you, I find it hard to put my thoughts into words.

I have fixed your passport picture in my cupboard at the side of the mirror. As you are looking straight into the lens, your eyes follow me wherever I am in sight of the picture! At certain times (I'll leave you to guess which), I find it rather amusing!

How are you rehabilitating yourself? As the days go by you will feel better. Anyway, I *do* think of you, Paul, lots and lots!

Love, from Stephanie

◆   ◆   ◆

Akron, May 8, 1949
Dear Stephanie,

Well, I think I am a little more organized now, and I shall try to write a little more sensibly in this letter.

After making enquiries about what I can send in a parcel to England, I guess I can send just about anything. They've just cut the postal rates in half for packages to Europe, so I have no excuse for not sending you things. By the way, it would be better to send food parcels direct to your mother at Merstham, wouldn't it?

As far as my photographs are concerned, some flaky little spots are appearing on some of the negatives. I have taken some rolls to be commercially developed—if they come back the same way, I intend to write to the manufacturer, and at least have them replace the film. The sad thing is, they can never replace my pictures!

I have been home a full week now, and I can proudly say that I am $50 richer. After I get out of debt—which shouldn't take more than two weeks—I ought to be able to put away $40 a week easily.

Guess what? *The Red Shoes* movie has come to Akron, and my friend Dennis and I went to see it last night. I really enjoyed it, and as I said, the ballet alone made it worth seeing. When the scenes outside Covent Garden were shown, I boastfully told Dennis that I had walked along that very place just a few weeks ago!

And so my darling, I've survived one week without you. How many more weeks will I have to get through before I see you again?

Bye for now, Paul

◆   ◆   ◆

Merstham, 8th May 1949
Dear Paul,

You say I've got to write you lots and lots to try and straighten you out. I don't want to make you feel any more miserable than you have been feeling of late, but I think it is better to have a few honest facts straightened out before us.

First of all, you say you love me. I believe you use that word superlatively. I don't want to be hard, but think—you were here for just a month, living amongst very different people and circumstances. I was with you most of that time, and therefore you didn't have much opportunity of getting to know any other English girls. And I think that if you had, your affections for me would have been less prejudiced. If you had met me in America, and I had an American accent, you would have not thought about me twice.

When I asked you why you loved me, you couldn't really say. "Because you're you," you said, and went on to remark about my liking Shakespeare and music. Well, that's nothing. At school here, we are brought up on Shakespeare, and if I had been able to say I didn't like his work and give a critical account of why I didn't, that would have been far more admirable. Anyway, Shakespeare is only one person, and put him on one side and the people I have never read or know about on the other, and the difference would be frightening.

I am not writing lots of meaningless sentences, but what I really believe in and which you will probably come to believe too. I am quite sure you haven't really thought it out, but have just got one idea firmly fixed in your mind, which, I think you could easily remove if you gave the whole situation a lot of consideration.

It isn't that I don't *want* you to love me, but that if you come to the point of closely examining it, you would find that it isn't love at all, but foreign emotions brought on by unusual circumstances.

I think I have said enough for the moment. Have I made you feel better? I hope I have.

Yours, Stephanie

◆   ◆   ◆

Akron, May 15, 1949
Dear Stephanie,

Here I am starting out my Sunday morning with a letter to you. I hardly know where to begin, but I guess I'll give you the good news first.

I now have my color film back and enclosed you will find a sample transparency. They're wonderful! I only regret that I didn't take more of them!

Now for the bad news. Twelve rolls of the black and white film are ruined by those flaky spots I told you about. It's enough to make one sit down and cry! Oh, I don't want to even think about it!

How am I rehabilitating myself? Time has a way of healing all ills—I'm back in the old rut again. I must ask you to forgive me for allowing such a lapse between letters, but I really and truly haven't had any time.

I have been doing some figuring about the future. I have written to some schools of photography—I want to find out what the tuition fees are and about how much it would cost me to live while attending school. If I could get by with spending only about $1000 at school this winter, I would still have enough to come to England by next April. Do you think I should go ahead with photography?

I'm going to sign off at this point, with the promise of a letter tomorrow or Tuesday.

Bye for now, your Paul

♦   ♦   ♦

London, 19th May 1949
Dear Paul,

I have been meaning to write several times this past week, but somehow I didn't have any go in me to do so. Every time I thought, "Oh, what's the use of writing letters—I'm sick and tired of writing letters that don't convey a thing." So I just waited until I collected some news together.

Thanks for the colour transparency—you are right, it certainly *is* wonderful! I do think the bad news about the spots on the film is just about the worst thing to happen.

I was interested to read about the photography schools you have been writing to. I think you really must go all out to enter one of these schools and put off coming to England until you have finished.

Now for your question as to sending a food parcel. Well, if it isn't too much expense or bother, we should be very grateful indeed. Your idea of sending it straight to Merstham is a good one. I haven't told my mother, so that it will be surprise. Oh dear, this paragraph makes me feel I am a sort of beggar—I suppose it isn't put very well. Anyway, I do thank you very much indeed, and just send it when you feel like it, because I don't want to be an obligation!

Remember the General, my mother's employer at Merstham? He has a new car now, and everybody is very pleased with it. Many people have come to admire it—it being a more or less up-to-date 1937 Rover, reconditioned, repainted, etc. It certainly is much better than the other one he had.

Yours, Stephanie

P.S. Reading back over this letter it appears to be just awful. If it weren't for the fact that I wouldn't have the stamina to write another, I would tear this up. As I said, I just don't feel inclined to write lately, so please give me some encouragement. I'm in the "what's the use" frame of mind. I can't see any point in sending these idiotic, newsy letters. I am beginning to feel it would have been better to have finished off the correspondence when you went back.

◆   ◆   ◆

Akron, May 22, 1949
Dear Stephanie,

I didn't work on Friday because of rain, and I thus had a chance to really get to work in my darkroom. I've got quite a few prints done, and might possibly finish up this week.

Another thing I did was to get a parcel ready to send to you. I've included two boxes of soap and two more pairs of nylons. I hope you like them—I think they're pretty sharp!

You must forgive me for not writing more often and for writing such poor letters. When I get home from work I'm dead tired. After supper, I come up here to my room and usually start to write to you—I write about three lines, tear up the paper and fling myself on the bed. Lying there, I ask you to forgive me. I wonder if you have the same trouble in writing. I tell you though, my main trouble is that I've been too tired—sometimes I just ache all over. Having this long weekend has done me a lot of good—I feel much better today.

Much better but for one thing! Why don't I hear from you? I suppose you have been finding it difficult to write too—at least I hope that's all it is!

Have you done much reading since I left? I haven't had time for much except my darkroom. The books are piling up on my desk!

I mailed off a food parcel yesterday—it will probably take five or six weeks before you get it! I have found an excellent food package service here in Akron to use the next time. They have a variety to choose from, and the order is sent airmail to Denmark, where the package is made up and shipped to Britain. It never takes longer than ten days!

I do wish I'd hear from you more often. Your letters are very important to my morale. I've been absolutely lost this week without even one!

Write soon! Your Paul

◆   ◆   ◆

Akron, May 23, 1949
Dear Stephanie,

I received your letter of the 19th today and I'm certainly glad to know that you're OK, and that you've just found it difficult to write. I know exactly how you feel. I must admit that our correspondence isn't what it used to be, but time will help—I'm sure it will.

You say it would have been better to have finished off the correspondence when I left. I too felt like "What's the use?" for a while, but I see things differently now.

I'm completely in the dark as to how you really feel about me. I think you really aren't sure. I wish I'd been nicer to you when I was in England, but then I didn't realize how much I wanted you for my girl. Then when I woke up, I couldn't talk—I couldn't say anything! You know how it was that last night!

Anyway, we said goodbye for a while, not forever! It won't be longer than a year before we meet again—I'm sure of that! So we must keep on writing—we must live and work for the future. In the meantime I can be doing things for you—sending you things and writing as often as I can. Oh, Stephanie, it really won't be too bad, and in no time at all we'll be together again. Make up your mind it won't be long and it won't be!

You know what vision of you I cherish the most? It was the morning of the day I left, when you met me in the record shop—remember? When I turned around and saw you there, you looked so sweet and beautiful! You were more serious than I had ever seen you, and I was glad because I felt you really cared.

Please, Stephanie, tell me that you are my girl, and that if we work hard and write lots of letters, in no time at all we will be together again!

Goodnight, my sweet, Paul

◆   ◆   ◆

London, 23rd May 1949
Dear Paul,

Once again I am groping for the right words to begin. This time it's harder than usual because I am feeling more than sorry for the last letter I wrote. I really don't know why I was in such a rotten mood, and then finished off everything by writing that childish P.S. I know really why I was so horrid was because I hadn't heard from you for some time until that day, but that's no excuse at all and only goes to illustrate how selfish I am, because in the letter I received from you today I read that you are usually too tired after working all day, which is of course very understandable. So now I am full of remorse. Will you forgive me?

The Philadelphia Orchestra is in England now. They are playing before the Queen tomorrow night and they played at Birmingham last night. I heard half of the concert on the wireless and it was magnificent.

Did I tell you about Wolfit's *Hamlet?* The whole time I watched it, I couldn't help but compare it with the film, and realize how near perfection Olivier came. The man who took the part of Hamlet was good in that he was energetic, clear and understandable, but his voice lacked distinction, and I couldn't take much interest in Prince Hamlet and his emotions. On the other hand, I thought Rosalind Iden was superior to Jean Simmons as Ophelia. The King and Queen were very weak indeed. In the part where the Queen is describing Ophelia's death ("There is a willow grows aslant a brook") well, that should have been moving and compelling, but she couldn't have any less expression in it if she had been saying "Ba ba black sheep." I think really that was the fault of most of the cast—they seem to be reciting nursery rhymes and not giving the impression that the words they spoke had just formed in their minds.

Philomena has just asked me to go out for some coffee and it is an invitation I can't resist. It's nice to imagine you think of me sometimes. Until I write again, I will say adieu and—cheer up!

Much love from, Stephanie

◆   ◆   ◆

Akron, May 28, 1949
Dear Stephanie,

Sunday morning again. Tomorrow is Memorial Day, and thus a holiday from work.

I received your letter of the 23rd yesterday, and I'm glad you've had a change of heart about writing letters. Of course I have forgiven you for your previous letter—don't waste any more words apologizing.

I mailed off a packet of my England pictures this week. You should receive them in about two weeks' time I should think. I have all my color prints back, but they are of poor quality and I am returning them to the finisher for a better job.

Your account of Wolfit's *Hamlet* was interesting—a nice piece of reviewing!

I have made up my mind to spend no less than three months in Europe when next I come. I want to visit France, Germany and Italy—as well as Scotland and Ireland. Every week as I page through the travel section of the *New York Times*, I feel all a-jump inside. I think that's the only real ambition I have in life—to travel!

Will sign off at this point, with a promise to write again soon.

Bye for now, Paul

◆   ◆   ◆

London, 2nd June 1949
Dear Paul,

Thank you for telling me of the Memorial Day you had last week. I noticed Monday was coloured in red on the calendar you sent, so I thought it was something special.

The other day I was walking down Gower Street, coming from the office, when I noticed a blind woman who seemed to be rather in difficulties. So I asked if I could help her along, and consequently took her home to her flat in Russell Square. She asked me to come in for a cup of tea, so I thought I might as well. She told me she was 82, and was once an artist. She showed me lots of pictures of herself when she was on the films in Hollywood! (Yes, really!) I didn't believe her at first, but when she showed me the stills, I did. There were pictures of her with Myrna Loy, Greta Garbo, Brian Aherne, William Powell and Donald Meek. She used to take tiny bit parts—mostly snobbish English-Hollywood aristocrats. She kept me talking for four hours! She lives all by herself and seems very lonely, so I promised to go along and read to her sometimes.

I was interested in your plans to visit the Continent. That of course can be discussed later, but for goodness sake don't make the mistake of visiting too many countries in too short a time—you won't get to see anything that way.

Do you ever get *Saturday Evening Post*? If so, do you think you could send me one across? I would also be obliged for another *Seventeen* if you ever get hold of one.

I was reading "Don Iddon's Diary" in the *Daily Mail* the other day, and it reminded me to answer one of your questions more fully—why I started writing to you in the first place. It was in "Iddon's Diary" that I read about the American Middle West, and he suggested it would be a good idea if English people would correspond with Middle Western folk. Another of my reasons was that quite a few of my friends had pen pals, and it really became quite a hobby (although most of them have thrown in the sponge by now). Earlier I wrote to girls in Belgium, Finland, and Newfoundland, but they all fizzled out eventually.

Until next time, Stephanie

◆   ◆   ◆

Akron, June 12, 1949
Dear Stephanie,

Another week has crept by, during which I received your letter of the 2nd. That was quite an adventure you had with the blind woman. Who would have dreamed what a past she has had!

Yesterday I sent you some magazines—*Life, Seventeen* and *Mademoiselle*. I'll send you some *Saturday Evening Post* magazines later this week.

A year ago you wrote me that I was pretty sharp to join the National Guard to stay out of the draft. Now that there's little danger of being drafted, I am trying to get out of the Guards. I have sent in an application to the New York School of Photography, giving my starting date as the first of August. When I have confirmation of this, I can take it to the Guard authorities and ask to be discharged because I will be leaving the state. I may not start school that early, but I want out of the Guard as soon as possible!

I wonder if you realize how important your letters are to my morale. I wonder too, if your feelings toward me have changed lately. Why don't you talk more about us in your letters? Of course I want to hear all the news, but if only you would finish up by assuring me that you do think of me and wish for me—that you do want us to meet again. It would make me feel ever so much better!

Your own, Paul

◆   ◆   ◆

London, 15th June 1949
Dear Paul,

You know, yesterday I told myself I shouldn't write you a letter for ten days or more. This morning I received a letter from you, and here I am replying to it straight away! I don't know whether it's more than you deserve, after not replying to my last letter for ages; I'll leave that for you to judge. I myself can't decide whether it's strong-minded of me or weak-minded—the latter I fear!

You ask me why I don't talk more about "us." I have purposely avoided that subject of late. I just don't want to say anything I will regret later on.

Do you know, sometimes I find it very hard to believe that you were ever here at all—it seems all a long way away and dreamlike. When next you come I shall be a different person—I want to too. I think I shall be very sophisticated! Anyway, doesn't it occur to you that we hardly know each other at all? If I am to include "absurdities" in my letters then they will be absurdities and not what I truly feel. I don't want to go on saying, "I miss you," etc. I think what the matter really is, that in my innermost heart I really don't believe you! Am I callous? I hope you don't think so. I just want to be honest, and really, I don't know what steps to take next!

Until later, I remain ever yours, Stephanie

◆   ◆   ◆

London, 18th June 1949
Dear Paul,

First and foremost I must tell you that your parcel has arrived! My mother received it exactly half an hour before she went away for her holiday! Mum was thrilled with all the things and will be writing to thank you soon, I expect. At the moment the food stuff is hidden away, but she sent the nylons and some Oxydol on to me, which I received yesterday. The nylons are beautiful, Paul, they really are—they are a wizard colour and so fine! Thank you, thank you, thank you very much indeed!

Oh it is such a lovely day today—I wish you were here to enjoy it with me. Next summer is such a long way off isn't it? What will you do when you meet me next time you come? Will you kiss me or shake my hand? Though of course if you come to the Club you will have to shake my hand, anyway.

You don't seem to be writing much these days, do you? I sort of expected a letter this morning, but there wasn't one. Ah well…

Yours with love, Stephanie

◆   ◆   ◆

Akron, June 20, 1949
Dear Stephanie,

Your letter of the 15th arrived today, and I am braving the heat here in my room to answer it immediately. I shall go straight to the subject I have been waiting to hear from you about—us.

First of all, we'll do it your way from now on—no "absurdities" in our letters—that's the way you want it, and that's the way it will be! I do think you are very cruel and heartless!

As for saying things that you might regret later on, that's silly. If one followed that rule strictly, one wouldn't say much of anything! As for me, I haven't said anything I didn't honestly and sincerely mean, and I am sorry for nothing I have said!

I suppose the memory of my visit has long since faded from your mind. I, of course, can never forget a moment of it! You say that when I come next time you will be a changed person—more sophisticated. That's the trouble now. You're too darned sophisticated—too English! You won't give way to your emotions no matter what, and if you do, you are eternally ashamed of yourself!

Why should you be ashamed? You know, over here girls go with a fellow for a week, swearing they will never love anyone else. Next week they are saying the same thing to somebody else! The boys are the same, but you won't find either the boys or girls sorry for what they've said and done. When a guy is kissing his girl goodnight, he doesn't stop and say to himself, "I've never felt more in love in my life, but I hardly know the girl—what if in two months' time I should decide I don't like her?" No, he doesn't want to think of such things—after all, he isn't deciding whether or not he is going to marry the girl—time will answer that question. And if nothing ever comes of it, he hasn't lost anything—he had gained in experience and enriched his life.

You say we hardly know each other at all. Quite true, but that won't stop me from wanting you. Perhaps you are right in spite of all I say, but I want you to know that the "absurdities" are still there, even if not written—and I still pass away the time of day with visions of you.

I really should tear up this letter, but it's done me good to let off some steam. Anyway, lecture's over! I must give up at this point—the sweat is running down me in streams! I thought I'd pass out at work today from the heat. I don't know why I work so hard when I don't have to. I guess I'm just a glutton for punishment—like you drinking hot tea on a day like this!

Bye for now, Paul

◆   ◆   ◆

Akron, June 21, 1949
Dear Stephanie,

After reading you letter of the 18th, which I received today, I'm sorry for what I wrote last night. I felt very downcast, lost and lonely after reading yesterday's letter, but now I'm sitting on top of the world again! You can be mean and cruel—but also sweet and loveable!

I am amazed you received the parcel so soon! I would like to send you some other things in the way of clothing, but I know how difficult that would be. Let me know what you think.

I fear that you are right. I haven't been writing very often lately, have I? Now that I have completed my darkroom work, the only excuse I have is this terrible heat. Sunday mornings are best, when my room is reasonably cool.

Do me a favor and forget all about my yesterday's letter, will you?

Good night, my sweet, Paul

◆   ◆   ◆

London, 23rd June 1949
Dear Paul,

I received a batch of magazines yesterday, including a *Holiday* and a *New Yorker*. I haven't had time to go through them yet, but with regard to the cutting you enclosed about the way we dress, it did make me mad—madder than I suspect you think! I marvel at your complete lack of taste and tact in sending it.

I don't think that man (the author) can generalize in that he says it is not just a lack of money, but that we English have no instinctive feeling for clothes. As it happens, there are quite a few reasons why we are a lot of old frumps, and, as you have made me so furious, I might just as well bore you with some of them:

For the last ten years we have "made-do" with the most miserable stuff we could lay our hands on. We didn't care about fashion at all because we had just enough to keep ourselves comfortably clothed. We grew up hardly hearing the word "fashion" at all.

From the age of 5 to 16 we are plunged into school uniforms, which we wear every day during school term. Lipstick, perfume, jewelry, etc., is of course forbidden, and perms are frowned upon.

We have no large-scale factories to mass-produce clothes to a standard compared with yours. Each manufacturer works separately and the hat producer couldn't give a damn what the handbag manufacturer might be making—just as the dressmaker couldn't care less what the coat maker is doing. We are fortunate indeed if we find anything to suit anything else.

Advertising of clothes is very poor, so we haven't many examples that we can copy.

Actually, I don't see your point in bringing up the subject. As for the reporter who started all this, judging from his description of glaring print frocks, floppy hats and large bows, I gather he spent all his time down in Piccadilly!

Well, that's that! I hope you don't think I've harped on the subject for too long, but I'm in such a temper, I couldn't care less.

Bye bye for now, Stephanie

◆   ◆   ◆

London, 24th June 1949

Dear Paul,

Yesterday evening and this morning I received your two letters of the 20th and 21st. In your second letter you asked me to forget the first, but I shan't. It was perfectly logical and you gave me what I deserved. You put things very clearly, and I suppose I am "too English." I see now I've been taking things too seriously, and I feel much easier now.

I suppose by now you have received the letter I wrote yesterday. Well, I shan't apologize at all for it because I meant every word! It's all completely finished in my mind now. You know though, our letters lately seem to have succeeded in making us both very miserable! Well, that's over and done with, and I am only going to say nice things from now on—I hope!

I received a batch of pictures from you last evening. Isn't that a lovely picture of St. Catherine's Point? And I loved the one of the sea too, but doesn't it look near? It looks as if we were on the beach and not on the cliffs.

I have worn one pair of the nylons you sent, and they certainly are "pretty sharp." Everyone likes them and has remarked on them. The colour is so attractive too! And so sheer! When I hang them on the towel rail to dry, they don't look like stockings at all, but just shadows of stockings!

Thank you for offering to get me other things sometime—you really are very sweet! Perhaps one day I might pluck up courage and ask you for something, but not until I have sent off the books you have requested.

It really is a scorcher here today! I don't know what I should have done without the nice hot cup of tea I had this afternoon to refresh me!

By bye—lots of love, Stephanie

◆   ◆   ◆

London, 27th June 1949

Dear Paul,

This is really an "in between" to tell you I have received the five packages of enlargements. The weather here is stifling and I'm sitting on the roof of the Club. I wonder if the heat in Akron is as intense as it is here—it's uncivilized having things so hot!

Now the pictures: Words are inadequate so how can I possibly say how beautifully you have done them. They are beautifully mounted too—you must have gone to a great deal of trouble and I really do feel awful for taking up so much of your time. However, I do so much appreciate them and the memories they recall. I only wish you were here with me so we could look at them together.

I like the one of the cloisters at Canterbury and the picture of Stoke Podges Church. The pavement artist also is good—that's one of my favourites. All the Stratford pictures came out well, and you have caught the ruins of Kenilworth and Warwick wonderfully.

"That letter" you wrote a few days ago has sort of woken me up I think, and I see things more clearly. I'm glad you wrote it—you put things very well you know! Anyway, you make me sort of miss you more than ever and make me sort of want to love you too! Shall I do that, Paul? Shall I love you?

Until I hear from you again, I am yours, Stephanie

◆   ◆   ◆

Akron, June 30, 1949
Dear Stephanie,

I really better start by excusing myself for the long gap between this and the last letter. I hope you aren't too furious with me!

Most of your earlier letter is concerned with the comments on the clothing issue. I think you are making a mountain out of a molehill. I am sorry I brought the subject up and will have to be more careful in the future.

Gee, I don't know how to write a fitting answer to your letter of the 24th. I'm glad you feel the way you do, and I hope that from now on we will stick together like pepper and salt, with no more arguments.

I suppose you get tired of me complaining about the heat and using it as an excuse to cut my letters short, but honestly, Stephanie, this weather is getting me down! Anyhow, darling, rest assured I am always thinking of you. There are so many things I should include in this letter, but am so tired and hot! So will you let your poor Paul "climb into bed, turn out the light and kiss my pillow—making believe it's you?"

Nighty—nite, Paul

◆   ◆   ◆

Akron, July 3, 1949
Dear Stephanie,

Once again it's my favorite time of the week—Sunday morning. As I sit here typing this letter, cool morning breezes are coming through the windows and a string quartet by Schubert is playing on the radio.

I wish, how I wish, that you could be here today. This afternoon we are going on a picnic somewhere along Lake Erie. This is our 4th of July weekend, so I'll have another day off work tomorrow.

Last week I went to the Liberty Theatre to see a film called *Louisiana Story*. There was a preview article about it some time ago in *Life* magazine, and the critics seemed to like it. I myself thought it rather pointless except as a good advertisement for Standard Oil, who had the film produced. But there was some good photography, and my favorite New York music critic and composer, Virgil Thompson, wrote the background music. On the same program was Hollywood's version of a recent American novel about the slums of Chicago, *Knock on Any Door*. The story is similar to *Studs Lonigan*, but is even more tragic in its ending. Humphrey Bogart is very effective as the lawyer, and as a whole the film is pretty good—for Hollywood!

Your birthday will be rolling around pretty soon, and I want to send you a little present. I'd like to send you a pair of those new nylon gloves the stores are selling—and I wonder about those blouses all the girls seem to be wearing. It shouldn't be hard to please you there, because they are very simple in design and are solid white in color. So please let me know your sizes!

Your own, Paul

◆   ◆   ◆

London, 7th July 1949
Dear Paul,

Thank you for your latest letters. As a matter of fact I did think you were dead or that a brick had fallen on your head!

It was your Independence Day the other day, wasn't it? I couldn't help thinking about you when I was typing 4th July on the top of every letter at work. I read somewhere that a few hundred people get killed every year in the U.S. on Independence Day—was it a rough house in Akron?

I can now see how ridiculous I have been about not wanting your letters to be more than mildly affectionate. You were so terribly brutal in "that letter" that you made me realize that if our letters continue in a platonic sort of way they will become dull and boring—I might just as well be writing to my Granddad as to you!

When you come over next year we shall soon find out how we really feel. When I read what you said about "having it my way," and just ending up "Yours, etc.," I felt sort of sad. Woman is fickle, isn't she? Anyway, now I do want you to say nice things to me and say you love me, because I do love you—lots and lots.

Yes, I did make rather a mountain out of a molehill about the fashion article, didn't I? Attribute it to the beastly frame of mind I was in. Perhaps I just wanted to get mad at you, and there was an excuse.

I saw *Letter To Three Wives* the other day and it was amusing. The second feature was some terrible thing about the American Forces in the Burma Jungle. I've never seen such sentimental rot in all my life! Remember how amazed you were at hearing one of our soldiers begging another soldier's pardon when we were at Dover? ("Even soldiers are polite in this country," I believe you said!) You would be even more amazed at these "heroes" patting each other on the back, gulping back their tears, and saying things like, "Yuh did a great job of work up there, son—the folks back home sure are proud of you!" When an American woman walks into their station from out of nowhere, they are all as nice as pie and the evening ends up with them singing hymns—aw nuts!

One night last week—the hottest I think we experienced—Gill and I were awfully brave and took our mattresses out onto the roof and slept there all night. It was most enjoyable too—one minute there were stars high above us, and the next minute there was the sun coming up over the chimney pots.

In regard to your sending me something in the way of clothes for my birthday—I wonder if I could say yes. Oh, Paul, it's awfully difficult, isn't it? After all, things are off the ration, but you do tempt me with those wonderful American things! It's funny you should mention those blouses, because they were forever catching my eye in the magazines you have sent. If you could find something very simple and typically American (no frills or off-the-shoulder necklines!), I would be very grateful. Oh dear, I must tell you the size though. Ah well—34" bust—now I feel awful!

Oh! What I should have mentioned last time was the food you sent! We had the chicken on Sunday, and it was scrumptious! It just melted in the mouth! As for the wieners, I might as well tell you, we were greedy and had them at the same time. They were rich too and actually tasted of meat, which I can't say for our sausages. Yes indeed, they really were scrummy and the like of which we certainly haven't eaten for ages! Thank you so much, Paul my love, I really am very grateful.

All my love, Stephanie

P.S. Do all your American girls look as wonderful as those gorgeous models in *Seventeen* magazine?

◆   ◆   ◆

Akron, July 10, 1949
Dear Stephanie,

We had a nice picnic on the 4th of July weekend, but it would have been so much better if you had been here with me. Oh, Stephanie, when shall we see each other again? I am beginning to doubt if I can live another year without you! I'd give anything in the world to have you here with me. Do you think it would be possible for you to accept a vacation in America at my expense? Oh, it's probably silly, but I wish for you so much!

You are right about people going wild here over the holidays. Over the weekend we had 737 deaths in this country—most of them on the highway, but some by drowning.

At the present time our papers are full of reports on Britain's dollar crisis. I fear that the way they play it up, most Americans have given up Britain for lost. They make it sound serious—and I guess it is—but maybe not quite as bad as they say.

I had a letter from your mother, telling me all about the "feast" you had from the food parcel—she was afraid you hadn't written to me about it! Anyway, it was nice hearing from her, and I'm glad you enjoyed the food as much as I hoped you would!

As for your comments on my wanting to send you items of clothing, it isn't that I feel I *need* to give them to you—after all, I was in England, and I know that you don't desperately *need* anything. But, being an American, I "figger" that it would be kind of nice if you *could* have some of the luxuries we enjoy. I also think you deserve it for putting up with so much "austerity" for so long! And besides, I love you and want to do things for you. As for the blouses, why are you so darned conservative? What's wrong with frills and off-shoulder necklines?

In answer to your question, do all American girls look as wonderful as those in the fashion magazines—the answer is, of course not! But on the whole they're a pretty good-looking lot—always neat, presentable and well dressed.

Goodnight my sweet, Paul

◆   ◆   ◆

London, 16th July 1949
Dear Paul,

It's Saturday night about ten. The others are downstairs listening to *Saturday Night Theatre*, but I've heard the play twice before, and I'm not bothering with it anymore.

This afternoon I saw *Yellow Sky*, and I *did* enjoy it. It was a typical Western and some beautiful scenery was included. While on the subject of films, if a certain picture called *Whiskey Galore* comes your way, move heaven and earth to see it. I did the other night. It's about a small island of the Hebrides, and how a ship carrying 50,000 cases of whiskey is wrecked near the island one night. The story is how the islanders manage to defy the army stationed there and get all the whiskey off before it sinks. It's funnier than *Passport to Pimlico*. I read somewhere that its title will be changed for your benefit to *Tight Little Island*, for fear that *Whiskey Galore* might offend Middle Western mothers!

As far as the dollar crisis you talk about, there always seems to be one as far as I've noticed. At the moment our papers are full of the Dock strikes and Railway strikes which have hit the country very badly these last few weeks. On Monday the King called a "State of Emergency," whereby the army stepped in and took over the strikers' work. It's pretty awful, isn't it?

In answer to what you say regarding my visiting America—Oh, Paul, darling, I would love to come. It would be wonderful! But it isn't practical, is it? I love you, Paul, I'm sure I do, and I want to be where you are, but it doesn't seem quite right. Anyway, I love you for asking me—you really are sweet!

About the blouse—I know I should like something very plain and neat, with a small collar maybe, and possibly some of that eyelet hole embroidery (which, incidentally, is not to be seen over here, and would be unique). And I'm not conservative! Low-cut necklines are horrible anywhere. Only one type of person wears them here—the Tottenham Road tarts! You need only to wear one of those necklines down Tottenham Court Road, and you've had it! So please, dear Paul, something plain, prim-prim, huh? By the way, won't you feel at all embarrassed having to purchase it? Or haven't you thought about that aspect?

Oh yes, I received the colour enlargements. They are beautiful! They take my breath away! I showed them to "the boys" at the office and they refused to believe that they were genuine colour pictures!

The authorities have discovered an unexploded bomb near us, and University College has had to be evacuated. We just escape the danger zone.

Goodbye for a little while. Remember I said I love you, and I do!

All my love, Stephanie

◆   ◆   ◆

Akron, July 24, 1949
Dear Stephanie,

I had just about given you up for lost when finally the postman bought me two letters today.

As for the blouse, I have already made a purchase! It's nylon, it's white, and it has a small collar with a very cute little ruffle around it. It's very thin and transparent, and I'm wondering if it will be O.K. Most all the girls around here are wearing blouses like this one—although I think this is the nicest I have seen.

I heard about the unexploded bomb on a BBC *Radio Newsreel* program. I thought of you at the time and wondered how near it was to the Club.

It means a lot to me to know that you do want me as much as I want you. I have made up my mind about one thing—if you won't let me bring you here, then I must give up photography school and all the rest and come to London as soon as I have sufficient funds. I can't help it—having you thousands of miles away from me is driving me insane! Life is so short and time is so precious! I must come to you!

It's a hot, miserable summer day, and I don't think I have ever been so disgusted with the summertime. One day drags into another—all dreadfully alike. Ah well...

I'm going downstairs to escape the heat. I think I'll have some ice cream and listen to some Mozart. I wish you could be here to help me enjoy them!

Bye for now my darling, Paul

◆   ◆   ◆

Farnborough, 30th July 1949
Dear Paul,

Are you wondering why I haven't written for ages, or have you been thinking the post office is at fault again? Last week I didn't write because I only received one short letter from you, and this week I received about three, I think—and the week just flew by.

Just lately I have wanted so much to be with you. I love you, and I want to be with you in America. But what's the use? I can't, and that's that! You are so far away, I can't imagine how far it is—sometimes I can imagine as far as New York, but from then on is a blank—everything is so remote.

In one of your letters you mentioned the blouse you have bought. It certainly sounds wonderful, and it will give me infinite pleasure to wear it, because it is American, because it's from you, and when wearing it I will feel much closer to you.

This is Bank Holiday weekend, and I am staying with my friend Anne in Hampshire. It is very nice down here and we are both in the garden in hammocks. At least she—I am half in and half out, trying to write legibly (I hope!).

All my love, Paul darling, Stephanie

◆   ◆   ◆

Akron, July 31, 1949
Dear Stephanie,

I see that I am going to have to have words with you! From now on, you are to write to me no less than twice a week—and no excuses!

I bought you some nylon gloves and will be sending them along with the blouse by air parcel post. They don't weigh much at all, so it shouldn't cost much to go by air—that way, you'll be sure to receive them by your birthday.

Looking over my future income and what I have saved so far, I am trying to decide what to do about coming to England. I should have something like $1200 by the end of the year. If I go to photography school at that time, I probably wouldn't have enough to come to England until June or July. The other alternative is to come to you in the spring and delay school until summer. What do you think?

Darling, I do hope I hear from you soon, Paul

◆   ◆   ◆

London, 3rd August 1949
Dear Paul,

With regard to your suggestions about coming to England again, I have studied them thoughtfully, though probably from a perfectly selfish point of view. I wish you would come for a month or six weeks in November and December. It would solve such a lot of problems, and we should really discover whether it's love or not. Oh, *do* come at that time if you possibly can, Paul. Oh it *is* the best plan, I'm sure! It seems far wiser than waiting so long, doing nothing more than writing letters and not knowing what our feelings really are.

The gloves sound "pretty sharp," but air postage does sound extravagant. How long do you think it will take the package to reach me? I have a *Times Literary Supplement* to send you and will do so shortly.

Much love, Stephanie

◆   ◆   ◆

Akron, August 4, 1949
Dear Stephanie,

We've got to work out a plan—and soon. The most important thing is how much we want each other. For my part, I'm sure in my heart that you are the girl

I want to love and live with forever. There's no doubt in my mind about that! Oh, Stephanie, my sweet darling, do you think you would like to be my wife? I don't want to put you on the spot about the future, but at least you know how I feel about you.

I still wish you could come here, but the more I learn about visa requirements, the more impossible it seems. Oh, Stephanie, I love you so! I shall just have to give up everything and come to you at Christmastime!

You must forgive me for this short note, but for the present there doesn't seem to be anything more to say.

All my love, Paul

◆   ◆   ◆

London, 8th August 1949
Dear Paul,

Your latest letter gave me a lot to think about. There is only one thing for you to do and that is come to England again, so that we can straighten things out more. Will you be able to come in December, do you think? Even if we do fall more in love and have to face another goodbye, I don't think it would be nearly as bad as this indecision which we are in at the moment.

And marriage! Dear Paul, is that what you really want? Do you want to have that millstone around your neck at twenty? I've never given it much thought—it appears to happen to lots of others, but I've never wanted it to happen to me—at any rate not for years and years.

But then, I love you. Sitting here in my room at the Club, I can think of nothing at this moment I should like better than to be with you. For some senseless reason or other, I wish more than anything I could turn around and find you here. Darling, you must come!

I am reading a book by Erskine Caldwell at the moment—*Tragic Ground*. Some of the language is quite shocking, but mostly it just makes me laugh. I never knew there were people *that* poor in America. It seems awful—Erskine Caldwell's people seem to be like animals.

I am vexed to see you haven't read many books lately. You must do something about it. Aren't there any Penguins I can send you?

I hope I hear from you again soon, my dearest Paul, Stephanie

◆   ◆   ◆

London, 11th August 1949
Dear Paul,

I have received the blouse and gloves! They are beautiful! I have never seen anything like them before. The embroidery on the blouse is perfectly exquisite, and the gloves are so fine and delicate I will not dare to wear them. They are the sort of thing Princess Margaret wears and "good little girls" who go to church every Sunday morning. But I shall wear them—this very weekend. I thank you so very, very much!

Last night I went to a Prom, and golly it was wizard! It was a Mozart and Schubert concert, with Richard Strauss thrown in for good measure. The best thing of course is that admission is only 2s. if you go in the Promenade. The snag is that you have to stand during the performance or sit on the floor, as there are no seats in the arena. There is a pool and a fountain in the center, surrounded by flowers. I only wish you had been there with me to enjoy the performance.

I think I had better finish off at this point and bid you a fond goodnight. Thanks once again for the very beautiful presents.

All my love, Stephanie

◆   ◆   ◆

Akron, August 12, 1949

> *June suns you cannot store them*
> *To warm the winter's cold,*
> *The lad that hopes for heaven*
> *Shall fill his mouth with mould.*

—A.E. Housman

Dear Stephanie,

I am starting a new feature to my letters with this one—putting some of my favorite quotes at the top of the page. Do you like this one?

I shall come to London in November or December, and I can stay for up to 60 days at the excursion fare of $466.70. I intend to make my reservations in about two weeks' time.

During those two months we'll be able to straighten things out. As for marriage being a millstone, I hope to change your mind about that. But we won't say any more on that subject now—we shall wait and see.

Do keep looking for a less expensive place for me to stay in London. I think I shall start sending you some pound notes to put by for reserve spending money.

What can I say for a final paragraph? Well, I love you—that's all! Will the day ever come when there will be no more final paragraphs—no more goodbyes?

All my love, Paul

◆   ◆   ◆

London 15th August 1949
Dear Paul,

On the *Third Programme* last night I heard a broadcast of *Antigone*. Oh dear, it did bring back memories of when we saw it at the Old Vic! Alec Guinness was Chorus, but he wasn't as good as Olivier. I still can't get over Olivier's complete naturalness, but Guinness appeared to be reciting a piece the whole time. Peter Ustinov took Creon's part, and I thought he was rather immature for the character—although, on the other hand, Mary Morris's voice was far too old for the youthful Antigone. I just can't think of anyone more suited to the part than Vivien Leigh. Still, I enjoyed the play immensely, with my ear glued to the wireless.

It's strange to think of it, but I wonder what will happen when we meet again. It's all right to sit here, several thousand miles away from you, and write saying how I wish for your kisses. But when the time comes, I'm sure I will be just too English and unemotional! Oh, hell!

I wonder if any of us will get any sleep tonight. It's so very hot! The barrel organ is going strong at the Pub at the corner and it will keep up the music until long after midnight.

Love and kisses, Stephanie

◆   ◆   ◆

London, 18th August 1949
Dear Paul,

Since last time I wrote, I have received several things from you, and this morning my mother telephoned me to tell me of a *certain intrigue*, which has been taking place. She told me she is in receipt of another parcel from you, which contained all the ingredients to make me a birthday cake. Oh darling, how very, very sweet of you! I shall have it at the weekend—but I wish you could be here to have a piece too!

Yesterday I received from you *The Spell of The Pacific*. It is a lovely book—just what I like to read—you couldn't possibly have selected anything better! Rupert Brooke, R.L. Stevenson, Herman Melville and others—it is going to give me many happy hours! Thank you ever so, ever so much!

I wore my gloves to Merstham last weekend, and everybody fell in love with them. I also took my blouse for them to see, which made them all envious. Erica (the General's daughter) said she is going to either kill me or scratch my eyes out—when I had the nylons she practically went mad, and now with the blouse she is nearly beside herself! It just goes to show, doesn't it, that with all her money, these things that I have are unavailable to her!

Miss Smith, the warden at the Club, is leaving. She gave in her notice because she hadn't been getting along with the House Committee. It is strongly rumored that the next warden is an ex-Women's Royal Navy officer, and we are all scared stiff!

The extract from Housman included in your letter I found amusing. He's a bad man to give people that sort of advice—leading them off the straight and narrow, but perhaps he's right.

I'm counting the days until you are here—I want you so much!

All my love, Stephanie

◆   ◆   ◆

Akron, August 22, 1949

Oh brothers, these sad tones no longer!
Rather raise we now our voices,
And joyful be our song!

Joy, thou spark of flame immortal,
Daughter of Elysium!
Drunk with fire, heav'n born Goddess,
We invade thy halidom!

—from Schiller's Ode to Joy

Dear Stephanie,

I feel like running through the streets, singing and shouting for joy today! I've heard that everything arrived safely for your birthday, and I have made my plane reservations for England! On Tuesday, November 22, I shall board an American Airlines Stratocruiser airliner in New York, and should arrive in London the next morning at 8:00 AM your time. I'm so excited! Only three months to wait!

So, Miss Grant, you think you'll be cold and unemotional when we meet again, eh? That won't last long if I can help it! I admit that your formality and manner of speech may have been a little inhibiting when I was with you, but then my American ways probably had you wondering at times too! Anyway, when we meet in November, we won't need to say a word—a kiss will say it all!

All my love, Paul

◆   ◆   ◆

London, 25th August 1949
Dear Paul,

First thing is to tell you how much we enjoyed all the things in the parcel you sent. The ham was delicious, and we had two meals from it. The whiteness of the rolls and the cake was truly amazing—I wonder when we will have really white bread again? The cake was scrumptious and so was the fudge mixture. I took some back for the girls in my room. Thank you so much, Paul, darling!

There's someone across the road from here who's learning to play the flute! It goes on every night—thin, wavering little tunes floating on the air. There is also some would-be opera singer residing in the vicinity—crikey, the noise is terrific. When it becomes unbearable, I compete against her and screech as hard as I can!

It's much better being eighteen than seventeen, I think. There are drawbacks though: I must pay twice the amount I used to pay for National Health, and I get no bananas until I am seventy! (We can still use Sonia's ration card for bananas though, until she becomes 18!)

So you are all booked up! Gosh that's wonderful—and November isn't so far away is it?

All my love, Stephanie

◆   ◆   ◆

Akron, August 29, 1949
Dear Stephanie,

Can I get just a little mad at you? Not very much—just a little bit? Today I finally received a letter from you, for which I am grateful, but you kept me waiting so long!

Now that you're 18, you're only one year behind me. I'll soon take care of that in December, when I will no longer be a teenager! Anyway, may you live to a very old age—long enough to have bananas on your ration card again!

I went to see the film *Quartet* last night, and enjoyed it very much. Have you seen it? There are four stories by Somerset Maugham—and all very good. This was my first introduction to Maugham, and I think I'd like to read his books. The four stories in the film were so haunting—I've been thinking about them all day today.

My evenings are so lonely. You at least always have some company—and I'm sure that is a help.

All my love, Paul

◆   ◆   ◆

London, 29th August 1949
Dear Paul,

Thank you for the pictures you sent. Is that the "front porch" of your house in the background of one of the snaps? Is Hazel Street typical of your streets? It looks very pleasant. I like your family car too—what colour is it?

The new warden isn't much of a success, I'm afraid, and she certainly is laying down the law! When Gillian came in an hour late the other night, the warden said that was the third time in a week and she would report her to Mrs. Chesterton! Gill had only been late once and was very annoyed about it. Then, the next night at half past midnight, the warden prowled around the bathrooms and found Gillian sitting on the floor eating bread and chocolate spread!

"Food," she screamed, "At this hour!" She went on to say it is strictly forbidden! Also lately we have had the vice-warden creeping about the roof in her nightgown at all hours of the night, listening to what we were saying. Life is exciting these days!

I've used up my space, but I will write again very soon. I am always thinking of you and longing for these two and a half idiotic, inconsequential months to fly past.

Much love from Stephanie

◆   ◆   ◆

Akron, September 4, 1949

Oh it's a long, long while
From May to December,
And the days grow short
When you reach September…

—*September Song*

Miss Stephanie E. Grant!

Why don't I hear from you? On Friday I received two packets of magazines, for which many thanks—but oh, if I could only have a letter!

I noticed in one of the magazines you sent, there was an article on what the U.S. thinks about Britain's dollar crisis. Nearly everyone I talk to has no use for Britain—they say they're tired of footing your bills. Today in the *Akron Beacon Journal* there is an editorial to the effect that we should cut off all aid to Britain because it is being wasted in a silly socialistic experiment. I'm afraid most Americans don't know much about what is happening in the world—most of them have never been beyond the borders of their own state! Oh well, I at least have faith that there will always be an England.

Mom is in Buffalo, visiting relatives and friends. Ted, Dad and I are left here to hold the fort. This time, I'm making Ted do the cooking, but it appears as if I will get stuck with the washing at least once before Mom gets back!

Because of the Labor Day holiday, there will be no mail now until Tuesday. Hope I hear from you then!

All my love, Paul

◆   ◆   ◆

London, 5th September 1949
Dear Paul,

I seem to have got myself onto your bad books these last few days, haven't I? Both your most recent letters contain scolds for not having written. I can't understand it, because I thought I wrote several letters last week, and I hope to hear soon that you have received at least one of them.

The words of the song you quoted were appropriate. I think it is a very haunting sort of song, and I have always liked it.

We're having another heat wave. Yesterday I went with Audrey to the seaside—to Brighton. It was delightful and the air so very fresh. Remember when we went on the boat at Brighton? The sea is wonderful—wonderful. Couldn't you be a fisherman or a lighthouse keeper, Paul? If you were, I'd willingly live with you all my life! It must be glorious just to live by the sea for years and years, until you are all brown and wrinkled and salty and you and the sea are part of each other. It's much better than messing about in cities, remaining pale of face and cynical.

At Brighton we played with the amusements on the pier for a while and looked in those atrocious machines labeled, "What the Butler Saw," etc. You put your penny in, turn the handle and moving pictures appear. They really are shocking! We had quite a lot of fun looking at them. We got back to the Club at about half past twelve, and the authorities didn't say a thing about us being late. We think it will come this evening!

Well, I hope to hear from you soon to say you have heard from me lately and telling me that I'm in favor again.

All my love, Stephanie

◆   ◆   ◆

Akron, September 6, 1949
Dear Stephanie,

This evening when I got home from work, I found not one, but three letters from you! So now I'm sitting on top of the world again!

Thanks for the pictures you enclosed, taken at the Club. But why none of you? I'd much rather see you greeting the dawn on the roof than Gill! I'd settle for any kind of picture of you at the moment—even if you had two black eyes, hair full of burrs, and leaning on a pair of crutches! Oh well, it won't be long until I see the real you, will it?

I don't have a printed schedule for my flight yet, but the Stratocruisers are supposed to take only twelve hours non-stop. If that is so, I should arrive at London Airport around 8 AM—providing we are on time, and I doubt if we will be! I wish you could meet me at the airport—maybe you could be "ill" that day and unable to go to work.

That cutting you sent about the boy preacher from America currently in Britain, reminds me that I've never mentioned all the loony religious nuts we have in this country. You should hear them on the radio—it's unbelievable the way they go on! Sometimes I have fun at work, "preaching" to the guys at lunchtime—trying to save their "lost souls!" After about two sentences they start howling with laughter, and then they try to make out what a terrible sinner *I* am!

Only 77 more days! And the days are getting shorter—a good sign. September—October—November. We're getting there!

I will bring as many things for you as I can—also Christmas presents for your mother and sister.

I love you, darling. Write again soon, Paul

♦ ♦ ♦

London, 10th September 1949
Dear Paul,

I was interested in your comments on the dollar crisis. I don't know whether you should take much account of what the people around you are saying—the Midwest is famous for its isolationist views, I believe. It seems wrong to me that Ernest Bevin and Sir Stafford Cripps (Home Secretary and Chancellor of the Exchequer) should be going to Washington to beg for more aid. I jolly well hope it is refused. We would not see Britain dwindle away into nothingness. All we want is a government that will put the country first and not mollycoddling of the people. If we and the Empire work together, we shall be as great as we have always been.

I thought you would criticize the pictures I sent! I am in the one with Gill, but you can't see me. That lump in the foreground is me—all buried beneath the covers!

Just over two months to wait now. One foggy morning in the not too distant future, I shall wake up and say, "Ah, today Paul comes."

You really are nice, wanting to bring Mum and Sonia something for Christmas. Nylons would be best for my mother, and if you want to bring something for Sonia, perhaps one of those American sweaters, if it is not too expensive—otherwise, bobbysox or suchlike. But don't bother with a food parcel. We shall have ample here. The Food Ministry always allocates a little extra at Christmas.

All my love, Stephanie

P.S. I really am in a dilemma! I owe a bar of soap to several of the girls and can't pay them back because I keep losing my coupons. Please darling, could you help restore my honor by mailing me a few bars soon?

◆   ◆   ◆

Akron, September 11, 1949

> *Unreal City,*
> *Under the brown fog of a winter dawn,*
> *A crowd flowed over London Bridge, so many,*
> *I had not thought death had undone so many;*
> *Sighs, short and infrequent, were exhaled,*
> *And each man fixed his eyes before his feet,*
> *Flowed up the hill and down King William Street.*
>
> —T.S. Eliot

Dear Stephanie,

Brrrrrrrr! It's cold this morning—the fall is definitely here.

Yesterday I bought my New York-London ticket! Ten weeks from Tuesday is the big day!

I hope you have forgiven me for all the hollering I did about not hearing from you. I must try to increase my own output to pay you back for all the wonderful letters I have received from you.

I got up a little later than usual—it's almost noon already! I've got to be off to get the New York newspapers soon. I want to get back in time to hear the CBS symphony concert on the radio—they're doing the Vaughan Williams *London Symphony* today! At the moment I am listening to some chamber music. That's one of the reasons I love Sundays so much—we actually get a little classical music on the radio then!

I heard from your mother the other day. She says she hopes I will be spending Christmas at Greenacre. To which I say, "Natch—of course!" Since I am going to send (or have Mom send) a package with the makings of a Christmas dinner, I wonder if you and I could combine our cooking talents and "whip up the eats."

Ah, darling, when I scoop you up into my arms again, I'll never let you go! Never! It's such a short time to wait, and yet so long!

All my love, Paul

◆   ◆   ◆

London 14th September 1949
Dear Paul,

This evening I passed a lamplighter busy working, which clearly indicates that autumn is on its way in.

I received another letter from you this morning. I liked the quotation—it seems typical of T.S. Eliot. Many times I have seen that scene of streams of people flowing up the hill and down King William Street. It's intriguing to watch the thousands of city workers flowing over London Bridge—not a smile on their faces, and they look neither left nor right at the river—they just pour over the bridge to their offices. Mum said she sent you a card from Boscombe. They had a nice time there I think, and came back all brown, looking like Indians. They stayed at some sort of religious hotel, recommended by an aunt. At breakfast on Sunday morning, grace took about ten minutes to sing, with "God is Love" at the end of each line!

All my love, Stephanie

◆   ◆   ◆

Akron, September 20, 1949
Dear Stephanie,

So you need soap, do you? I'll send some off right away, *and* remember to bring some with me when I come.

I heard last week about the devaluation of the British pound. It goes without saying that I will benefit, but I can't help but wonder how it will affect you people. What are the reactions over there?

Dennis is talking of going to New York City—he has relatives there and goes every so often. When he mentions New York, I always say with a yawn, "Oh yes, I believe I make a stop-over there, en-route to London!" At that point, he picks up the nearest object at hand, and I get ready to duck!

Have I ever told you how much I love your handwriting? You are always apologizing for it, but you shouldn't! I never have any problems reading anything you write, and I never find it sloppy—even when you say it is!

I have broken the news to Mom—about my trip. As I expected, she is trying to argue me out of it. Of course she doesn't know yet how much I am in love with you, but you'd think she would have guessed by now, wouldn't you?

Nine weeks from today!

All my love, Paul

P.S. The pound is already selling here at the new rate—$2.80!

◆   ◆   ◆

London, 25th September 1949
Dear Paul,

Things at the Club are getting worse. The new warden is a real old battleaxe, with hair scraped back over her head, very upright of carriage, and a loud voice. None of us care for the "revised rules."

I haven't written for over a week, because several of us have been out in the evenings, looking at flats. On Friday, Audrey, Wendy, and I went to have a look at a flat in Notting Hill Gate, which is really in Kensington and not far from the center of things. It impressed us more than anything we had seen, so we took it! The rent is six pounds per week—with four of us it will be 30s. each. It's in the basement, and has two large rooms with coal fires and four divans, and it has its own front door. My mother says we are fools and will starve, and I'm beginning to feel a bit worried. It seems rather frightening to be leaving the safe and secure walls we know and start out on our own alone! Still, we have given in our notice at the Club, and by this time next week we shall have left for good and all. I'll send you the new address next time.

The devaluation of the pound did come as a shock, but judging from what I have seen around me, nobody seems to be caring in the slightest! Anyway—just rejoice that you will have more money for your trip!

I don't think it would be wise for me to try to meet you at the airport—I couldn't possibly go out there in the early hours of the morning and wait for goodness knows how long before the plane arrives. And if you are going to kiss me when you arrive, I should not think the American Overseas Airlines office in St. James Street is very practical! We will sort it out later on, I expect. Anyway, there will probably be a kindly November fog enveloping everything, so wherever you meet me, don't go kissing the wrong girl!

I'll write again soon darling, Stephanie

◆   ◆   ◆

London, 30th September 1949
Dear Paul,

This is just a short note to give you my new address: 18, Colville Square, London W.11. Everything is all right and we are now moving in. Gosh, isn't it wizard? We'll have our own little home with whatever meals we want to fix—we are going to have lots of salads and plates of spinach!

Bye bye for now. Write me soon at the new address. Hurry along November!

Until I hear from you again, all of my love, and I'm just longing for the time when you will be with me again.

Still love me? Stephanie XXX

◆   ◆   ◆

Akron, October 2, 1949

> *October has come again, has come again,*
> *And this world, this life, this time*
> *Are stranger than a dream.*

> —Thomas Wolfe

Dear Stephanie,

October has come again, and so has Sunday morning. It's a beautiful Indian Summer day—my favorite time of the year.

Reading over your comments on the new flat, I'd say it sounds ideal. If you can afford it, why not? It makes me a little sad, however, to think that you won't be at the Club anymore—I do have a memory or two of the place—especially the first time we met in the lobby!

I do want to see *Streetcar Named Desire* and *Death of a Salesman* when I come—also, I have heard good things about *The Lady's Not For Burning*. Let me know what other exciting things will be on.

If the customs man looks into my luggage, he is going to think I am a sweater salesman! Yes, I went shopping yesterday and got carried away! In addition to a sweater for Sonia, I bought three for you! One is a cardigan and the other two are pullovers. One of them is 100% white nylon, and is surely what the angels wear when they get a little chilly! I hope you like them.

The film *Pygmalion* has come to Akron and I hope to see it this evening. Wonder if I'll ever get to see Olivier's *Hamlet*?

All my love, Paul

◆   ◆   ◆

London, 4th October 1949
Dear Paul,

We're all settled in now, and it's wonderful! It's so much better than the Club, you can't imagine! Everybody had been very kind by way of bringing us things we need. My mother came up the other day, and I think, in spite of herself, she quite liked it.

Streetcar has opened in Manchester, and certainly startled the audience. At first they gasped, but in the end they cheered. The reviewer predicted the biggest controversy yet when it does come to London.

You know, I feel rather a fraud, because although I am home with a cold, I am going with Gill this evening to hear Beethoven's *Choral Symphony*. It's Furtwangler with the Vienna State Opera Orchestra. It's too good to be missed.

I'm so glad this letter is going today. If my surmises are correct, you will receive it on Monday next. Now if I had sent it yesterday, the receiving date would have been Saturday and you would have answered with your Sunday letter. But if you get this on Monday, you will probably write me again on that day! Don't you think I'm rather crafty?

Do I write enough about "us" these days? You don't complain, so I guess I do. I must now scrape myself some lunch together—spaghetti on toast, I expect.

Love and kisses, Stephanie

◆   ◆   ◆

Akron, October 10, 1949
Dear Stephanie,

It's Monday evening, and as you predicted, your letter arrived today. Since yesterday was a busy day for me, I didn't get around to writing my usual Sunday letter. So all your craftiness was in vain, wasn't it? Only one letter after all, instead of two! I'm sorry darling—I wish now I had written yesterday.

I hope your cold is better and that you enjoyed the Beethoven *9th Symphony*. I should think it was a very good performance.

I went to see *Pygmalion* the other night. It was *so* good! Leslie Howard was just great in that film, wasn't he?

I've been showing my England pictures to quite a few people lately—friends and relatives—and they do seem to be interested in what I have to show and tell. Once I get started, the words just seem to keep pouring out—amazing!

As to writing about "us," as long as you keep writing and telling me you love me, I won't complain about anything!

This is a shamefully short letter, but I must get it into the post as soon as possible, since I didn't write yesterday.

Goodnight, my love, Paul

◆   ◆   ◆

London, 11th October 1949
Dear Paul,

First of all, I must thank you for the sweaters you have bought for me. But goodness—*three* of them! I know you'll think I'm being silly, but I feel pretty awful! I do thank you very much—you really are a dear, generous boy!

I was interested to read about your showing people your pictures of England, and more still that people were interested in them. That really is quite a victory for you, because it seems that however enthralling an experience is for you, when you try to tell someone else about it, you can seldom be successful in interesting them.

The Beethoven *Choral Symphony* was thrilling. The soloists were particularly good. Gill and I were up in the Gods at the Albert Hall, so the music seemed to be coming out from the bottom of a well, but it came across perfectly.

We are still getting on very well at the flat. I didn't know housework was so hard. There seems to be such a lot to do. Vivien does most of the cooking, although I did cook some fish the other day. Ugh! I just hate dealing with beastly wet fish, especially when it comes to cutting off their heads!

It isn't long now until you come, is it? Just over a month in fact. I have booked seats for *Streetcar* on the first Saturday you are here.

All my love, Stephanie

◆   ◆   ◆

London, 16th October 1949
Dear Paul,

Thanks for your letter of the 10th. It wasn't a very affectionate letter, was it? Still, as you were very busy and obviously not really in the mood, I can sort of understand.

Enclosed please find a cutting about *Streetcar*. Personally, I've had rather a shock! I didn't think it was such a blatant, sexy play, but more of a poetical nature. I'm not so sure I want to see it now!

This is the day after our "housewarming," and none of us had more than three hours sleep last night. Paul, dear, I wish you had been there last night—of one thing it made me more certain, and that is I like you more than ever! Silly isn't it, but there it is. Darling, you are a dear, sweet loveable boy, rather young, but I love you very much. Do you still love me? Do you know, in your letter, I even doubted it!

I feel somewhat without a muse, and the radio is blaring forth. Please forgive me if I finish now.

With all my love, Stephanie

◆   ◆   ◆

Akron, October 20, 1949

> *Up in the morning,*
> *Out on the job,*
> *Work like the devil for my pay;*
> *But that lucky old sun's got nothin' to do*
> *But roll around heaven all day!*

—Popular song

Dear Stephanie,

I don't remember my letter of the 10th being particularly unaffectionate, but if so, I am very sorry about it. Our letters have been a bit dull lately, but that's because we haven't had any arguments and are just biding our time until that magic day in November. However, I intend to remedy the situation—this letter will be different!

Glad your housewarming party was a success. I wish I could have been there to enjoy it with you, although I am not really fond of parties as a rule. It's you that I am most fond of, and I want you all to myself—far away from everybody else!

I have a surprise for you. This Saturday I am mailing off a package with soap (bars and flakes), a box of cocoa, and some chocolate candy kisses. Save me a few of the soap flakes though, so I can wash my new nylon shirt.

Are you having fun reading this letter? I told you it was going to be different! [Ed. note: Alternate paragraphs were typewritten upside down.]

I really feel badly that my letter left you sort of doubting my love. It's frustrating trying to send love in a letter, but when we're together again, you'll see that there's no room for doubt! Meantime, darling, I love you, uoy evol I—anyway you look at it—I love you!

Goodnight, my dearest, Paul

◆   ◆   ◆

London, 20th October 1949
Dear Paul,

I tried to write yesterday, but I hadn't a muse—and I haven't one tonight. I don't know what's the matter with me. I know as sure as anything I am to be fired this week. It's my entire fault because I haven't concentrated on anything for ages. Oh, I just can't seem to concentrate on anything at all!

It's funny isn't it—you say you love me and you don't really know me at all. I don't suppose you ever imagined I was so lazy, incapable, and so generally wretched a creature.

I hope you don't mind my going on like this, but it's been refreshing to pour my heart out to somebody. I feel so low at the moment, and I should think you will consider twice about coming to England on my account.

Paul, darling, if you can, write me some encouragement! Tell me how to think again and how to stop being so lazy. From now on I shall take life far more seriously. I feel awful for not having written anything more important. Our letters these last few weeks seem to have dragged, haven't they? I wish you would hurry up and come!

Think of me sometimes—all my love, Stephanie

◆   ◆   ◆

London, 24th October 1949
Dear Paul,

I received a very delightful letter from you this morning, and I must answer it straight away. It really was terribly funny to have half of it upside down—I wondered what on earth was happening at first! I haven't had such a nice letter from you for ages, although I am beginning to think I don't merit your words of loving kindness!

Thank you for all the things you are sending. I shall certainly have enough soap to last me now. The chocolate kisses sound scrummy. There is a popular song doing the rounds now—"candy kisses, wrapped in paper…" It always makes me feel hungry, and now I shall get to know what they taste like.

I have booked you a room at the Cumberland. I should think it will be quite easy to find somewhere cheaper once you are here. I am going to do some theatre bookings this weekend, starting with *The Lady's Not For Burning*, and perhaps an opera. The Old Vic is doing *Love's Labour's Lost* and *She Stoops to Conquer*. Where possible, I shall aim at paying no more than 10 shillings. What else shall I book?

Thank you again for that lovely letter.

Yours with love, Stephanie

◆   ◆   ◆

Akron, October 24, 1949
Dear Stephanie,

Your letter of the 20th arrived yesterday. I agree that our letters have not been very exciting lately, but then, that's the way it goes. When you don't have a muse, letters are a chore and a duty, but at other times writing is sheer delight. When you think about it though, we both have a right to get discouraged now and then—after all, we've been writing to each other now for a year and a half!

I'm glad you did pour out your heart to me in your letter—I love you all the more because you did. Losing your job is not going to be the end of the world, and as for feeling lazy, I get that way lots of times! As for the future, let's wait and talk about that when I am with you again.

Only four more weeks darling, and there will be no more misery for either of us! Cheer up—I do love you so!

Your own, Paul

◆   ◆   ◆

London, 28th October 1949
Dear Paul,

I received your letter in reply to my "outburst." I am an idiot, aren't I? It was a dear, understanding answer you wrote, and far more than I deserved! I shouldn't have written such a miserable letter, but there it is—I did.

Anyway, everything worked out all right in the end and I wasn't fired. As a matter of fact, they told me today I am to have another girl to help as the work is getting too much for one person!

Oh, Paul darling, I do love you and want you to love me. I suppose everyone gets a feeling of depression sometime or the other. Anyway, that's all over now, and I feel secure again.

It's only just over three weeks now—imagine! I hope it's a fine day when you arrive. There are some good operas on at Covent Garden, and I have written for seats for *The Magic Flute* on November 24th. Does that meet with your approval?

All my love, darling Paul, Stephanie

◆   ◆   ◆

Akron, October 30, 1949
Dear Stephanie,

Gosh, but I'm having to work hard on the job these days! No rest for the wicked!

Dennis and I went to see a French film the other night—*The Chips Are Down*, from a story by Jean Paul Sartre. It concerns the deaths of a man and woman during the occupation of Paris. They didn't know each other during life, but meet after death and fall in love. They appeal to the authorities to be able to return to life—claiming they were destined for each other. They are permitted to do so, but they must prove their love for each other. If they do so, they will be allowed to live out the rest of their natural lives together. They think this will be easy, but in the end, they fail—and die for good. The scenes where they are dead are wonderful fantasy! They still inhabit the earth, but cannot be seen, heard, or sensed in any way. The whole film is very well done, and typically French in its impact. Loved it!

I went nylon shopping yesterday. I got some nice ones for your mother—a shade called "Woodsmoke." For you, I got some more of the "Picturesque" nylons, in a new and fancier style.

My own wardrobe is rather shabby and inadequate—pretty much what I brought with me last time.

Only three more weeks! It's hard to believe, isn't it? I'm feeling that old excitement again—sometimes too excited to go to sleep at night.

See you soon, my darling Paul

◆   ◆   ◆

Akron, November 2, 1949
Dear Stephanie,

I'm glad to hear that you are over your "outburst" and that things are going well for you now. From here on in we won't talk about anything depressing, will we? We love each other and nothing else in the world matters!

A thousand hugs and kisses for booking *The Magic Flute*. Can you also book for *Boris Godunov* at Covent Garden on December 2nd?

My money situation doesn't look too good—it looks as if I will have to get along on about two pounds per day. I can't stay at the Cumberland long at that rate, can I? Oh well, I think it will all work out.

Forgive me for signing off so soon, but I've got darkroom work to do. I've done some portraits for a friend, and that means a little extra money for my trip.

All my love, sweet Paul

◆   ◆   ◆

London, 14th November 1949
Dear Paul,

According to your strict instructions, I am writing this last letter today so that it will reach you safely before your departure. There are a few important developments to tell you about.

First of all, I have all next week off! I shall spend two glorious days resting at Merstham, then return to London Tuesday evening. And the following day you will arrive! I should think the best thing you can do now is to proceed immediately to Colville Square, as soon after you arrive as possible. I will draw a little map to enclose with this letter. Don't forget that it's an area basement, so look out for the steps going down past a number of dustbins, mangy cats and old milk bottles, and you will arrive at our door!

I hope you will have a wonderful journey. Don't miss the plane! Oh, Paul darling, I'm getting so excited! May this week just whiz by!

All my love, Stephanie

P.S. Seven kisses.

◆   ◆   ◆

Akron, November 17, 1949
Dear Stephanie,

This will be my last letter before seeing you. Oh, darling, the big day is almost at hand! I'll be so excited when I board that plane, they will think I am crazy!

To date, I still don't know how to get to Colville Square, but I am sure a map is on the way. Never fear though, I will find you! In all probability, I shall be in London about noon, but when traveling by air it is best to be prepared for anything. If you take off on time and arrive on time, your ancestors were surely Irish!

Darling, next Tuesday my life will begin again, and this existence I have had for the past six months will disappear like a bad dream. Between now and then, I want you to hate everybody and everything as much as possible—that way you'll just be bursting with love when I knock at your door!

Oh, Stephanie, I love you so much!

Your Paul

◆   ◆   ◆

If either Stephanie or I had any lingering doubts about our love for each other, they dissolved into nothingness when we were reunited on that joyful day in late November 1949. We were married in London on January 6, 1950.

There was one more brief separation when I returned to America to await the approval of Stephanie's U.S. visa. During this six-week period we wrote to each other daily, longing for the time to come when there would be "no more letters between us—ever!"

More than fifty years later, we are still together—still in pursuit of the knowledge, joy and magic we have always found in reading, music, and the theatre, the common interests that brought us together all those years ago.

There have been no more letters.

Following their 1950 marriage in London, Paul and Stephanie set out to build a life together in Akron. Paul decided to remain in construction work and took up the trade of bricklayer and stonemason, which had been in his family for three generations. Stephanie used her secretarial skills to help support the family and to finance a college education for herself. Upon receiving a master's degree in history, Stephanie taught English at Kent State University and eventually became a lecturer in Western Cultural Traditions at the University of Akron.

The Dukes live in rural Medina County (just west of Akron) in an English stone cottage that Paul built in 1955. They have a daughter, two sons, two granddaughters, and one great-grandson.

In 1980, Paul decided to retire from construction work and realize a long-cherished dream to become a dealer in old and rare books. With Stephanie's assistance, he operated the business out of their home, a portion of which was converted into a bookshop. Ever the Anglophile, Paul called the business "Cotswold Corner Books," and he made frequent buying trips to England for old and cherished volumes. For both Paul and Stephanie, whose passion for books was instrumental in bringing them together in the first place, the business was an appropriate and fully satisfying activity, which they continued until 1995.

The Dukes have turned their retirement years into a time of writing books instead of merely selling them. Stephanie has written up her wartime memoirs, *We Won't Know Where We're Going 'Til We're There*, and Paul has undertaken the task of editing *Dear Stephanie, Dear Paul*. Both have been working on various family history projects, which involve seemingly endless research and writing.

Acknowledgements

Quotations in the letters came from the following sources:

Collected Poems of A.E. Housman
Henry Holt, N.Y. 1940

Crane, Hart, *Collected Poems*
Horace Liveright, N.Y. 1933

Eliot, T.S., *Collected Poems 1909–1935*
Harcourt, Brace & Co., N.Y. 1947

Huxley, Aldous, *Jesting Pilate*
Chatto &Windus, N.Y. 1926

September Song
Lyrics by Maxwell Anderson and Kurt Weill, 1938

That Lucky Old Sun
Lyrics by Haven Gillespie and Beasly Smith, 1949

Wolfe, Thomas, *The Face of a Nation*
Literary Guild, N.Y. 1939

978-0-595-39505-7
0-595-39505-8

Printed in the United States
64742LVS00002B/103-174

9 780595 395057